big sky
cooking

big sky cooking

**MEREDITH BROKAW
AND ELLEN WRIGHT**

PHOTOGRAPHS BY
TOM ECKERLE AND TOM MURPHY

ARTISAN | NEW YORK

Published by Artisan
A Division of Workman Publishing, Inc.
708 Broadway
New York, New York 10003-9555
www.artisanbooks.com

Library of Congress Cataloging-in-Publication Data

Brokaw, Meredith.
Big sky cooking / Meredith Brokaw and Ellen Wright.
p. cm.
ISBN 1-57965-268-9
1. Cookery, American—Western style. 2. Cookery—Montana. I. Wright, Ellen. II. Title.

TX715.2.W47B75 2006
641.5978—dc22   2005055869

Printed in Singapore

10 9 8 7 6 5 4 3 2

WE DEDICATE THIS BOOK TO THE SPIRIT OF MONTANA: its respect for nature's bounty, its wilderness, its wildlife, its incredible open spaces, and the generous people who live there: Doug and Karen Campbell, John and Katherine Heminway, Bob Jackson, Larry Lahren, John Lounsbury, Val Lovely, Tom and Laurie McGuane, Nan Newton and Dave Grusin, Susan Pauli, and Stacie Stengle.

Thanks also to all the people throughout the country who helped us: Grace Benjamin, Jessica Benjamin, Meg Bloom, Dennis Brady, Sarah Brokaw, Anna Bugallo, Julie Coburn, the Betsy Hambrecht/Robert Eu Family, Caren Ezratty, Jennifer and Allen Fry, Joslyn Hills, Kristi Jacobson, Geri Jansen, Carla Jegan, Soni Karp, Robert Karp, Kristin Lemkau, Gerda McDonough, Elizabeth Picsik, Stacie Pierce, Claudia Plepler, Alexis Proceller, Michael Radin, Jean Rather, Monika Rozec, Andie and Charles Simon, Liam Stokes, and Chip Wallach.

CONTENTS

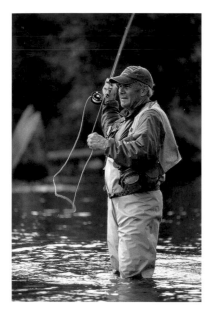

FOREWORD BY TOM BROKAW

THIS BOOK ABOUT FOOD, LIFE, AND FRIENDS IN THE AMERICAN West is the final chapter in a favorite Brokaw family story.

It began when I first talked dreamily about buying some land, maybe even a ranch, in Montana. Meredith, who had skied, hiked, and traveled with me throughout Colorado, Wyoming, and Montana, shared my excitement about the geography and the lifestyle but drew the line at making any kind of substantial financial or personal investment. It was all too far away from our home in New York, too much to worry about, and besides, when we felt the call of the West we could simply visit as we always had in the past.

"If you do this, Tom," she cautioned, "you'll have to take care of it. I have enough to handle at this end of the country."

Throughout our long, happy life together I have always trusted her judgment and tried to accommodate her wishes. But I had a severe case of Rocky Mountain fever, and the only way to cool it was to buy something, preferably a few acres and a cabin on a trout stream.

That, it turns out, is the single most difficult piece of real estate to find in Montana, so I widened my vision by a few thousand acres and bought into a beautiful ranch on a blue-ribbon trout stream in an isolated valley just north of Yellowstone Park.

For six months Meredith refused even to visit, despite my glowing descriptions and assurances that she would love it as much as I did. Our children and friends were amused by this small fissure in what had always been a common view of goals and passions.

Finally, I persuaded her to spend a weekend. I asked one of my favorite Montana ranch families to trailer over some horses so we could ride through the valleys of wildflowers and over the ridges rimmed with Douglas firs and massive boulders left behind long ago by the ice age.

At the end of a daylong ride, helping a neighbor move cows from one pasture to another, Meredith looked at me from atop her horse and offered her first reaction. "We could go back to New York, sell everything, and just move here," she said.

We didn't go quite that far, but in the intervening years our western life has been the perfect complement to the hurly-burly pace of New York, network news, board memberships, writing books, and jumping on airplanes for far-off places.

Whenever we approach our ranch on a long, winding gravel road that crests a hill at a place called Wolf Point, our hearts skip a beat as the vast grassland, West Boulder River, the mountains of the Absaroka Range, the bison herd, a sky full of raptors, and wild game come into view. It never fails to be a humbling experience.

That perspective, that here nature rules, is a constant during our time in Montana. We mark our days by the bison calving season, the summer storms that nourish the grass and demand slickers on horseback rides, the insect hatches that feed the trout, the health of the grouse and partridge coveys, the elk migration, and the first sighting of bear or mountain lion. We eat wild game harvested during hunting season, catch and release rainbow, brown, and cutthroat trout, talk cattle prices with neighbors and surround ourselves with a menagerie of dogs, cats, and horses.

When night comes late in the day the big, black sky explodes into a panorama of stars and constellations, a great arc of light that is the only illumination as far as we can see.

It's a privilege to be a small part of this great American landscape and to share it with you.

HOMECOMING BY MEREDITH BROKAW

OUR MONTANA RANCH HAS FELT LIKE HOME FOR SIXTEEN YEARS.

To my initial surprise. Although my husband and I tend to agree about most big things, I was apprehensive about buying property so far away from our East Coast lives. But Tom was smitten by the land and the landscape. He promised to take care of everything from afar—rather like a child promising to take full charge of a puppy—and he prevailed. When he went off to Montana for the closing, I had the fleeting thought that this could be the pilot episode of a TV sitcom.

We'd owned the ranch for six months when I visited it for the first time. It's on a dirt road, well known for its washboard bumpiness, seventeen miles from the nearest town. It was June and, despite the snow higher up in the mountains, the grass carpeting the basin far below was Ireland-green and swaths of deep blue lupine swept over the slopes. It was breathtaking.

I grew up on the Great Plains in the neighboring state of South Dakota, so my arrival that day had a resonance for me; I had a very real physical sense of homecoming. I'd adapted well to life in the metropolitan East, but now I could feel my western self reawakening. I spent the day exploring the beautiful land and, to put it mildly, the ramshackle buildings on the property. The spread seemed to have grown up in an unguided or, at least, misguided way. One building was white, another red. One barn had been painted forest green, and another a dismal brown. Aesthetics aside, electric wiring was strung all over the place and looked to me like a makeshift job, not only unsightly but also dangerous.

But the truth is that by the end of that first day I knew, sitcom moments notwithstanding, that owning the ranch would turn into a love story, and it has. We soon discovered that this wasn't just a place to inhabit; it was a world of its own and a way of life. For example, it

seemed odd to use the word *neighborhood* to describe an area where the houses aren't within sight or even walking distance of one another. To our delight, though, we had indeed moved into a neighborhood of sorts, even if our neighbors aren't the kind from whom you can quickly borrow a cup of sugar. We were curious about them, and they, of course, were curious about us. One by one, we met them, people who were either Montana born and bred or who were drawn here from other places, as we were.

When you live in a remote place, you're maybe even more drawn to company, and because meetings are less frequent, each becomes something of a celebration. Hospitality takes on a new meaning when someone drives forty miles to have dinner at your house, never mind just to stop by and say hello. In due course, we began to figure this out, and to find our friends, who helped us learn the cadences of Montana life.

We also brought our world to Montana. The ranch has proved to be a great gathering place for our three daughters and their families, my brothers and sisters and their families, and Tom's mother and two brothers. Like most of America, we no longer all live in the same town or even in the same state. We keep track of one another's major life events, but we don't see one another regularly. The ranch became our remedy—or, more precisely, Camp Runamuck, a loosely organized and usually rather chaotic event that every two years brings together as many of us as possible for a three- or four-day reunion. Runamucks are always packed with horseback riding, canoeing, hiking, and fishing, as well as huge family meals that, for me, have a sense of ceremony.

Our friends come, too. Ellen, who is my good friend and coauthor, is the quintessential example. We met nearly thirty years ago when a mutual friend introduced us. But that was in New York, and Ellen is an East Coast girl through and through. The first time she came to visit in Montana, I realized that much of life out West that seemed ordinary to me needed translation for her—starting with vocabulary. Not many Easterners refer to their vehicles as "outfits," or add "You bet" as a sign of affirmation in conversation. Trail mix is called "gorp." Hens are "layers." And what was that "latigo" for again? (It's the strap that tightens a saddle girth.) But the city mouse thrived, and I've been amazed at what Ellen has created on her many trips since then.

Most visitors, particularly those who have just been released from the city, seem to stretch out and expand with the land; I do it myself, and I love seeing my friends experience it. Ellen's reaction was a bit different. I showed her the horses and the livestock and the wide-open spaces, and I could tell that she thought, Very nice. But when I showed her the chicken coop, and the girls who lay an egg per day, her eyes lit up. "Omelets, custard, potato," she said, her face brightening. The vegetable garden had the same effect. And when we left the sunshine for the dim light of the pantry, she grew positively radiant. "I love Montana!" she exclaimed.

Ellen is a food person, and she had found her own corner in this vast state. Over the years, she has brought her sophisticated flair to our simple fare, and added a touch of Montana's distinct and delicious cuisine to her own recipes—an East meets West fusion of sorts.

Montana is often called Big Sky Country, and for good reason. The horizon seems endless when viewed from the plains, and you can spot different weather patterns all going on at the same moment: a clump of clouds dumping rain to the south; sunny, clear blue heavens 180 degrees to the north. On a clear night, with no ambient light from any towns and at our elevation of 5,500 feet, the Milky Way appears to be a wide white ribbon stretched out overhead. You can almost touch the Big Dipper, Orion the Hunter, and Taurus the Bull. The universe feels so alive with shooting stars and orbiting satellites, and an ever-changing moon. I remember feeling alarmed the first time I saw a full moon emerging over Mount Ray, because I thought it was a forest fire coming up the other side. Even when the moon is a sliver in its first stage, it is a presence.

I think of the state as big in other ways, too. People come here with big dreams, and for the expansive possibilities the land offers. For years I thought about trying to corral these big appetites and this way of life into a book. Each year the idea became richer as Montana became more a part of our lives. Each year, too, my neighbors and friends have thrown their thoughts and impressions and bits of local lore—to say nothing of their recipes—into the mix. It was Ellen who finally said, "Okay, Meredith, let's do this book." Just like an old-fashioned barn raising, friends from miles around have had a hand in seasoning our collaboration, filled with recipes that were born here, or that were brought here, or that were transformed in and by Montana.

FRIENDSHIP BY ELLEN WRIGHT

IN THE FALL OF 1976, THE BROKAW FAMILY WAS MOVING TO New York, and mutual friends told them to call me. I invited them to dinner; they were living in a hotel temporarily, and I figured a home-cooked meal would be a proper welcome.

As Tom remembers it, I made guinea hen and lentils. We talked nonstop that night and haven't slowed down since. We love to laugh and tell stories; we share many common interests; and although we have different backgrounds, many of our core values are the same. First, our families are most important in our lives; our children are the same ages, and now we're both experiencing a great love affair with our grandchildren. Second, we love to travel, learn new things, and fully enjoy our blessed lives. And third, we appreciate being home, where we can invite our favorite people to break bread with us.

I've been cooking seriously since 1960, when I was in my early twenties. My training included French cuisine with Julia Child, studying with Claude Bailes of the Cordon Bleu, pastry lessons with Maurice Bonte, and Indian cuisine with Madhur Jaffrey, as well as working for James Beard doing demonstrations and testing for his books. While this rigorous education has served me well over the years, I have, now in my sixties, adopted a more relaxed approach to food and entertaining.

I remember Meredith's trepidations about the new ranch in Montana, but of course she came to adore this home of hers, and the more I heard about it, the more my curiosity was piqued. When I finally visited for the first time, I, too, saw it all: the magic of Montana.

That's not to say it didn't take some getting used to.

The pace was like a slow-motion movie to me. People seemed to mosey, not walk; saunter, not rush; amble, not charge. I listened to the

way people talked, in a kind of "nothing bothers me" tone—slow and deliberate, wary but not rude. I heard new cadences, new inflections, and new expressions. They'd say, "That deal won't pencil" about a bank loan or any plan or idea that would never pan out. A rider whose horse was spooked by a rattler would say, "My horse blew up." For me, it was like listening to a new language, a new song. I tried to slow down and emulate the rhythms, but my Eastern clock kept getting in the way.

Even though I'm from such a different part of the country, I feel a connection. I admire this nuts-and-bolts way of dealing with life, this direct and minimal way of talking and doing, this taking care of business. Montanans always seem to know how much rain falls every month and how much live cattle are going for and which neighbors are selling off their herd. They're always doing deals—horse-trading, piggybacking one deal on another, like coming to the ranch to dig a well

but offering to charge half their fee in exchange for grazing rights for their cows.

Montanans are also the champions of playing down bad situations. Tom told me about a cowboy who was charged by a bull in a rodeo competition. His leg was fractured so badly that the bones came right through his jeans. Three weeks later he was limping around the ranch when Tom asked him where his crutches were. "Can't ride a horse with crutches" was his answer.

Life on a ranch is tough. There's always a ton of work to do: caring for the animals, repairing the equipment, working the land, feeding the livestock. Then there's seeing to the house: cleaning, washing, laundry, grocery shopping, gardening, harvesting food that's ready to pick and planning meals accordingly. And things happen—a fence breaks and the cows get stuck on the barbed wire or get separated from their herd, an old bison bullies the group and has to be isolated or removed.

But no matter how busy life at the ranch is or how tired we are at the end of a long day, we all look forward to dinner. Every meal is meaningful, a time to talk about the day's events and to reward ourselves with good food and good company.

After writing two cookbooks, I thought I had tasted, or was familiar with, almost everything. Then I was introduced to the meats and fresh produce available in the West: bison, elk, antelope, chokecherries, and huckleberries, to name a few. I didn't realize how much I would learn, and it didn't take me long to love it all. With Meredith's passion for her ranch and my passion for cooking, we decided to write this cookbook so we could share our enthusiasm and tell the Montana story. We created many new recipes, retooled family standbys, and reinterpreted the classics. It's all simple, honest, delicious food, offered with great respect for hardworking people who take life head-on in a wonderful way.

RHYTHMS OF THE RANCH

EARLY MORNING IS A FAVORITE TIME AT THE RANCH FOR TOM and me. I'm up with the sun at 5:30 in summer, much earlier than my New York routine. It's quiet, except for the chatty magpies. I make my faux cappuccino—nothing more than French-roast drip coffee topped with milk whipped into a froth and heated in the microwave—and head out to the deck. Though Montana can get very windy, it's usually very still at dawn, and the combination of clear, sharp light over the soft colors of summer is powerful. In counterpoint, there's the ever-present rush of the river, only about twenty yards from my perch on the deck, but it feels like a background refrain and doesn't overwhelm these early moments. Our Labs, Sage and Abbie, keep me company as I plan the day.

Tom likes dawn as well—I guess he got used to it from all his years on early-morning TV—and he regularly gets up with me and goes out to his office in the "cave" for some uninterrupted reading and working time. The cave is actually a modernized old soddy—a log house with a sod roof—built into a hillside, the grass roof of which has been replaced by wood shingles; it was probably an ice house or a root cellar originally.

As the sun rises higher, the sandhill cranes fly over. They're always in pairs and call to each other with their distinctive voices. And that's when the rest of the household begins to wake up, too. Ours is a modern working ranch, but at this hour the up-to-date improvements we've made seem to have done little to change the templates of history. The place has had many lives and, at dawn especially, I can easily imagine them all.

Until a century ago, the Crow Indians used this land as their summer hunting ground. It was abundant with elk, antelope, and whitetailed and mule deer; it still is. The Crow are not forgotten—one of the old-timers in our area still steeps cedar needles in hot water to

make a medicinal tea for various ailments, just as the Crow did for centuries. And in summer the farmers' market usually offers rustic chairs, lamps, even beds and bowls made from the beautiful and durable indigenous cedar.

Sometime in the early 1900s, a Norwegian immigrant by the name of Tom Hoiland homesteaded the land and built a two-room farmhouse on what is now our property, though he never got around to nailing boards over the insulation batting in the kitchen; he'd finish eating and stick his knife and fork into the wall, ready for the next meal.

Subsequent owners raised cattle and grew hay, and in the 1980s the place became a small dude ranch. By the time we arrived, the farmhouse had a bigger kitchen, a bathroom, and an enclosed front porch.

Using local workmen, all of whom had a say in the process, we eventually added on to the main building, though it's hard to tell from the outside that much has changed; it just looks like a slightly bigger version of the same early-twentieth-century farmhouse. We built a long room whose windows face the river sixty feet away. Even though they're classic windows in keeping with the old style, there are ten of them, admitting cascades of early-morning sunlight and an intimate sense of the stream outside. At one end of the room is a TV and a couple of easy chairs. In the center, a sofa faces the fireplace, and at the other end, adjacent to the kitchen, there's a dining table with six mismatched chairs. If it's just the two of us, this is where we eat, to the refrain of the river.

We also renovated a second building, known as the lodge, which dates from the days of the dude ranch and functions as a gathering place. The kitchen, with a Garland range, two refrigerators, a large freezer, two dishwashers, and two sinks, can accommodate between twenty and thirty people for meals.

In its present incarnation, the ranch has about 125 head of bison and 16 horses. It's managed year-round by Doug and Karen Campbell, who live in a house on the property with their teenage daughter. They're both good cooks as well. Doug is a master with the grill and the smoker, and Karen, an art teacher by training, is very creative in the kitchen.

At about 6:30 in the morning, the ranch officially wakes up when Doug starts the four-wheeler to bring in the horses, which have been out all night grazing in one of the pastures. This process is quick if the horses are close by; if they're hidden down in one of the many swales, it can take a while to find them. Once they're in, Doug checks them all to make sure there are no missing shoes or injuries, then spreads some cake—compressed grain pellets—around the paddock as a treat. The chore list varies from day to day—tending the livestock, gathering eggs, repairing the barn and the fences, maintaining the machinery—but the grind of a diesel motor, from the tractor and the ranch truck, is almost a constant—so much so that we have our own diesel gas pump.

Ellen and her husband, Joe, once gave me the perfect hostess gift: a clock with a hook underneath. Written on the face of the clock is: "If my hat's gone, I'm out riding." The hat in question is my Stetson; I feel bare without it, and for good reason: from about noon till about four, the Montana sun is so fierce that you need constant protection and shade for your eyes.

At four, the ranch resumes its morning rituals, but in reverse. The horses are led back out to pasture, the machinery is put away and turned off, we raid the garden for our evening meal, and my hat goes back on its hook. That's when you'll usually find us in the kitchen.

IN THE KITCHEN

IN MY CITY LIFE THE FOOD CHAIN IS SIMPLE: MARKET TO kitchen to table, often with very little fussing in between. (Sometimes it's even simpler since there is an abundance of restaurants in our New York City neighborhood.) With the variety of ethnic everything so readily available, I've always found it a pleasure to cook and experiment at home. That usually involves daily stops at the fish market, the butcher, a couple of produce stands, the baker, and tucked-away, pocket-size boutiques for herbs and spices.

Things in Montana are entirely different. First of all, when you're seventeen miles from the nearest town you tend not to forget that quart of milk, so soon after we moved here I learned to run the kitchen not day to day but week to week, even month to month. The pantry is stocked for two to three months at a time with basics— flour, spices, canned goods—and the garden gives forth all summer with vegetables and herbs of all kinds. The freezers are all filled with bison and game, and the hen house is busy all the time, with each of the girls laying an egg a day. It's a whole different way of life, and I like it. Much of our sustenance comes from the land, and the kitchen is where we, not the shopping bags of exotic ingredients, make everything come together.

The cooking, too, is really basic and uncomplicated. Having fresh eggs, a garden full of lettuce, spinach, rhubarb, peas, asparagus, radishes, carrots, and so on is a bonus. Rather than focusing on how far away the supermarket is, I focus on what's ripened in the garden and is available on the spot to eat. Because our bison meat is organic and fresh and comes from our own land, we know that these animals have eaten nothing but grass. Or perhaps because we're more relaxed in these surroundings, food simply tastes better in Montana. We generally have meat for dinner four or five times a week; I keep a variety of cuts in our freezers. The other nights we have vegetables, soups, omelets, fish, or pasta; pasta puttanesca is one of my standbys.

Tom and I both enjoy fishing in the late afternoon and early evening; there's usually an insect hatch and the fish are eating, so it's a good time to catch them. We catch and release all the trout we hook in the river, but about once each summer we catch and release into the frying pan one or two trout from our pond. If I haven't planned dinner beforehand, putting together this quick-and-easy no-fuss one makes the fishing more fun.

We also often grill meat on the barbecue, with two and sometimes three vegetables with each meal—and I'm not even a Southerner! There are so many ways to prepare the same vegetable—steaming, roasting in the oven, sautéing, or sticking them on the grill with the meat—that it's hard not to seem like a genius.

When we renovated the farmhouse a few years ago, we were adamant about keeping the integrity of the original building, but at the same time we needed a working kitchen. The new room is a bit bigger, but you can still see yesterday in it. Our builder, Terry Baird, a native of the area, is incredibly skilled at finding and using old doors, hardware, and fixtures, which kept our renovation authentic. He built kitchen cabinets with old wood, covered the counters in copper, and used beadboard for wainscoting. My collection of chicken cookie jars lives on high shelves on two walls. And all my appliances, including my ice-cream maker, get a lot more use here than they do in New York. This is where I love to cook.

RANCH BREAKFAST

GRANGE GRANOLA

BACON AND EGG PIE

LALA'S CHEESE GRITS

VAL'S CINNAMON ROLLS

GRANGE GRANOLA

1½ cups canola oil

1½ cups honey

3 to 4 cups old-fashioned rolled oats

1 cup wheat germ

¾ cup assorted nuts (almonds, walnuts, and/or your favorite)

¾ cup assorted dried fruit (apricots, raisins, and/or your favorite)

Tom's favorite breakfast almost always includes Grange Granola. We're lucky if there's any left to stick in our pockets for hikes. There's some discrepancy about whose recipe it is. I say it's mine; Tom says it's his. But I know it's mine.

MAKES 15 TO 16 CUPS

Preheat the oven to 350°F.

In a medium saucepan over medium heat, combine the oil and honey. Cook until heated through; set aside.

In a large bowl, mix the oats, wheat germ, and nuts with the warmed honey-oil mixture. Spread the mixture about 1 inch thick on a rimmed baking sheet. Bake, turning the mixture a few times with a spatula, 20 to 30 minutes. Let cool. Add the dried fruits and toss to distribute well.

Store the granola in an airtight container for 3 to 4 weeks.

BACON AND EGG PIE

½ pound thick-sliced bacon

¼ pound mushrooms, sliced

1 yellow pepper, cored, seeded, and diced

4 ounces goat cheese, crumbled

⅓ cup grated Parmesan cheese

1 teaspoon chopped fresh thyme, or ½ teaspoon dried thyme

6 large eggs

1½ cups heavy cream

Kosher salt and freshly ground black pepper to taste

This is a good example of the simplicity of cooking at the ranch. When we're expecting guests for breakfast or brunch, we prepare the food the night before and refrigerate it. In the morning we bring it to room temperature and then bake it. For a crowd, the recipe doubles and triples very well.

SERVES 6 TO 8

Preheat the oven to 325°F. Butter a 10-inch pie plate.

In a large skillet, cook the bacon until very crisp; drain on paper towels and set aside. Discard all but 2 tablespoons of the bacon fat. Add the mushrooms to the skillet and cook over medium heat, shaking the pan from time to time, until browned.

Transfer the mushrooms to the prepared pie plate. Crumble the bacon on top and add the pepper, goat cheese, Parmesan, and thyme.

In a medium bowl, whisk the eggs lightly; whisk in the cream. Season to taste with salt and pepper. Pour the egg mixture over the mixture in the pie plate. Bake until the eggs are set and browned nicely, about 1 hour. Remove and cool slightly. To serve, cut the pie into wedges or use a serving spoon to spoon out individual portions.

LALA'S CHEESE GRITS

1 teaspoon olive oil

8 tablespoons (1 stick) butter

3 garlic cloves, minced

5 cups water

1¼ cups regular grits

3 large eggs

8 ounces extra-sharp cheddar, grated

8 ounces pepper Jack cheese, grated

kosher salt and freshly ground pepper to taste

Lala is Laurie Buffet McGuane, a sister of Jimmy Buffett. The whole Buffett family is into food. Jimmy created his Margaritaville restaurants, which are now all over the world. His sister Lulu's restaurant in Gulf Shores, Alabama, called Lulu's at Homeport, is famous for its gumbo. Laurie knows all about hearty western food but tips her southern hand when she entertains, especially when she serves this dish.

SERVES 6 TO 8

Preheat the oven to 350°F. Butter a 2- or 3-quart baking dish. Set aside.

In a small skillet over medium heat, heat the olive oil and 1 tablespoon butter. When the butter foams, add the garlic. Cook, stirring, until the garlic is lightly browned. Set aside.

Heat the water in a large saucepan over high heat until boiling. Reduce the heat and, with a whisk, slowly stir in the grits. Continue stirring until the mixture has thickened slightly; it should be the consistency of thick tomato sauce.

Cube the remaining 7 tablespoons butter. Add the butter to the grits, a few pieces at a time, whisking to get a velvety texture.

In a small bowl, lightly beat the eggs. Stir in a few teaspoons of hot grits. Pour the eggs back into the grits and stir quickly. Stir in the cheddar cheese, Jack cheese, and garlic. Season to taste with salt and pepper.

Pour the grits into the prepared baking dish. Bake on the middle rack until the grits are set and the center is solid, about 1 hour and 15 minutes.

The old Mercantile Company building in Wilsall has been home to Val's Deli since 1999.

THE NOT-SO-SECRET VAL'S DELI

I FIRST WANDERED INTO VAL'S FIVE YEARS AGO LOOKING FOR A quick sandwich after spending the morning at JayDee Anderson's arena. JayDee is a trainer of reining horses, and although I'm not by any means one of his better students, he's a patient coach, and I've had more than a barrel of fun riding there. The horses are all athletic and well trained, and JayDee's expertise attracts all sorts of people from the midsection of the state to the far eastern part. You never know who'll be riding at the same time you are, but it doesn't matter—JayDee has time for criticism and encouragement for everyone, and I'm always glad that I made the trip. It's about an hour's drive, but it goes quickly when my riding buddy Nan and I go together. And it was with Nan, a close neighbor who splits her time between Santa Fe in winter and Montana in summer, that I first discovered Val's.

When you step inside Val's, the first things you see are a few items meant to attract tourist attention—the requisite T-shirts and coffee mugs with an outline of the state imprinted on them and tags that proudly announce "Made in Montana." Past a couple of tables and chairs is the counter, where all the action is. (The tables get used only when all the places at the counter are taken.) Travelers on their way north to Glacier National Park or south to Yellowstone stop in at least occasionally (why else the merchandise?); I'm sure these drop-ins are surprised if Val is conducting her small game of chance when they order: "Wanna shake the dice to see who pays for the coffee? Double or nothing." Who can resist, especially when the coffee comes.

But I've seen only local residents having coffee or eating lunch. There are a couple of regular older women lunchers; most of the diners are men, cowboys who refer to themselves as ranchers, in dusty boots,

Wrangler jeans, Carhartt jackets when it's chilly, and well-worn cowboy hats that no one thinks of removing indoors. They're having their noon meal on a break from their tractors, mowers, pickups, and four-wheelers. They all know one another, and there's a lot of ribbing and kidding going on across the counter. Val participates.

Val Lovely is well known in the Shields Valley, a broad expanse of Montana grassland between two mountain ranges in the northern Rockies, the Bridgers and the Crazies. Val's husband, Larry, traces his roots here back to 1889, when Moab Lovely established a successful homestead. Larry and Val are carrying on the family ranching tradition, but like many Westerners they need additional sources of income. Val's solution was to open a café and call it a deli in the cow town of Wilsall, a friendly little community straddling Highway 89 and named after Will and Sally Jordan, the children of Walter Jordan, who laid out the town originally.

When I asked Val what prompted her to open a deli—which, by the way, doesn't resemble delis as I've come to know them in the East; there are no pastrami sandwiches, lox, or bagels anywhere near this one—she told me that her mother wondered the same thing. "I've never known you to cook!" her mother said. "How can you open a restaurant?" But Val pushed ahead, and it turns out that she can indeed cook. The locals are grateful for her hearty breakfast and lunch menus, including a daily special, served six days a week with a healthy side order of sass and local gossip.

The place is generally a two-woman operation, even when business is at its peak in the summer months. Val, a handsome woman who looks good wearing her bibbed apron over a T-shirt and shorts—necessary apparel for a hot summer kitchen without air-conditioning—is there

The Brokaw Labs, Sage and Abbie—a couple of range rovers.

most mornings, kneading the dough for her softball-size cinnamon rolls so they'll be ready with the coffee for the breakfast crowd at 7:30. (Throughout the farm and ranch country of the Midwest and West, fresh-baked, extra-large cinnamon rolls might as well be listed with the state bird, the state flower, and its most popular scenic attractions. Based on my own samplings, Val's are the best.)

As soon as breakfast orders are cleared, Val gets busy preparing "dinner," which is what the midday meal is still called in ranch country. It's a big meal for folks who have already put in several hours of hard work. The special of the day—meat loaf, pork roast, hamburger goulash, big burgers, occasionally, a chicken dish—is by far the biggest seller. When chicken is on the menu, Val knows what's coming from her cattleman crowd: "What part of the cow did that come from?" Montana may also be known as sheep country, and more and more bison can be seen on the grassy slopes of its foothills and basins, but beef is still the staple of the local diet. Val's burgers are exceptional. She buys ground meat, adds Worcestershire sauce, chopped onions, and a raw egg, and is careful not to overhandle the meat as she shapes the patties. She uses an extra-hot grill, and the burgers are at their finest when not rare.

That first day, Nan and I climbed up on the stools, studied the blackboard, and decided on our order. It was interesting eavesdropping on all the back-and-forth conversation while waiting for my BLT and Nan's hamburger, and we kept our conversation to a minimum in order not to miss anything. Since then, lunch at Val's has become part of my routine after many morning rides; my friends from the barn often meet there. It's also my restaurant of choice for lunch when we have visitors from the East because the experience is authentic and the food is good. I've sampled many of the offerings on the menu but keep returning to my very first, the BLT; by midsummer, the tomatoes are a true red, the lettuce is fresh, the bacon is crispy, and the whole-wheat bread is lightly toasted just the way I like it.

I thought Nan and I had discovered this little jewel when we decided to see what was inside the unprepossessing building on the highway with a handwritten DELI on the side wall. I soon learned that Val's is no secret. The new faces are now very familiar. My Montana neighborhood keeps expanding.

In the fall, the aspens turn a spectacular golden color, especially dramatic against the dark green of the pine trees.

VAL'S CINNAMON ROLLS

You won't face a long line at Val's Deli waiting for these rolls to come out of the oven at 7:30 if you make them yourself. Val's original recipe could feed an entire platoon. This version is more manageable.

MAKES ABOUT 18 ROLLS

1¼ cups whole milk

½ cup vegetable shortening

½ cup granulated sugar

1 teaspoon salt

2 cakes compressed fresh yeast, or 2 (¼-ounce) envelopes active dry yeast

4 large eggs, beaten

5 cups all-purpose flour

4 tablespoons (½ stick) unsalted butter, melted

CINNAMON SUGAR

½ cup granulated sugar

2 teaspoons ground cinnamon

TOPPING

1 pint heavy cream

¼ cup firmly packed dark brown sugar

¼ cup (½ stick) unsalted butter, softened

Heat the milk in a medium saucepan over medium heat until almost simmering. (The milk should make a spitting noise when you tilt the pan.) Remove from the heat and stir in the shortening, granulated sugar, and salt. Cool to lukewarm. Crumble the yeast cakes into the milk mixture and stir until the yeast is dissolved and the mixture is foamy. Add the beaten eggs and blend lightly. Add 4 cups flour and mix with a wooden spoon. Turn the dough onto a lightly floured surface and knead, adding more flour if necessary, until smooth and elastic, 3 to 4 minutes.

Shape dough into a ball and place in a well-buttered large bowl. Cover and place in a warm nondrafty spot and let rise until doubled in size, 1 to 2 hours.

Divide the dough into two portions and roll each to an 8- by 10-inch rectangle. Brush generously with the melted butter. Combine the ½ cup granulated sugar and cinnamon; sprinkle on the dough. Roll up the dough lengthwise. Slice into 1-inch-thick rounds.

For the topping, combine the cream, brown sugar, and softened butter in a medium bowl. Spread the mixture on the bottom of a 9- by 13-inch baking pan. Place the rolls in the pan, cover, and let rise until doubled in size, about 1 hour.

Preheat the oven to 375°F.

Bake the rolls until brown and beautiful, about 20 minutes. Remove and let cool before serving.

THE QUEEN'S BRUNCH

SMOKED TROUT
WITH HORSERADISH SAUCE

SAUTÉED SWISS CHARD

SAVORY BISCUITS

SILVER DOLLAR PANCAKES

FRONTIER EGGS

SMOKED TROUT WITH HORSERADISH SAUCE

Perfectly smoked trout served with zesty horseradish sauce on toasted thin-sliced bread with a squeeze of lemon is a taste worth pursuing. Smoked trout is sold in many specialty markets. We've also successfully smoked the whitefish caught in our river.

SERVES 6

2 pints sour cream

$1/4$ cup bottled white horseradish

4 (8-ounce) boned filleted smoked trout

4 lemons, quartered and seeded

4 to 6 thin slices black bread, lightly buttered and cut into quarters

In a pretty bowl, mix the sour cream and horseradish with a fork. Arrange the fish on a pretty board or platter. Serve with the sauce, lemon wedges, and buttered bread for guests to help themselves.

SAUTÉED SWISS CHARD

Swiss chard takes over our garden every year with its bushy leaves, just like a weed. Lightly sautéed with a little crushed garlic, it tastes sweet and clean—perfect with our eggs in the morning.

SERVES 6

1 large bunch Swiss chard

2 tablespoons olive oil

3 cloves garlic, crushed and minced

Wash the chard leaves thoroughly and discard the stems. Cut the leaves into 2-inch strips and set aside to drain. Heat the oil in a large skillet over medium heat until it is hot but not smoking. Add the garlic and cook, stirring, for 1 minute. Add the chard leaves. Cover and steam until the greens are wilted.

SAVORY BISCUITS

Fresh sage and chives add a savory taste to a basic biscuit recipe. I leave butter at room temperature so it's easy to spread on these piping-hot biscuits.

4 cups all-purpose flour

3 tablespoons sugar

2 tablespoons baking powder

2 teaspoons chopped fresh sage, or 1 teaspoon dried sage

2 teaspoons chopped fresh chives

   Pinch of kosher salt

1 cup (2 sticks) salted butter, cut into pieces

2 cups heavy cream

MAKES ABOUT TWENTY-FOUR 3-INCH BISCUITS

Preheat the oven to 400°F.

In the bowl of a food processor, combine the flour, sugar, baking powder, sage, chives, and salt. Add the butter and pulse on and off until the dough resembles coarse meal. Add the cream all at once and pulse a few times, until the dough comes together in a ball.

Place the dough on a lightly floured surface and gently pat into a 1-inch-thick round. With a 2- or 3-inch biscuit cutter, cut out rounds and place on an ungreased cookie sheet. Press scraps together and cut out additional biscuits.

Bake the biscuits until golden brown, about 20 minutes.

SILVER DOLLAR PANCAKES

2 cups all-purpose flour

1 tablespoon sugar

1 1/2 teaspoons baking powder

3/4 teaspoon kosher salt

2 cups milk

2 large eggs

2 tablespoons vegetable oil

Melted butter, for brushing the griddle

I grew up hearing the colorful story of my grandfather's encounter with Calamity Jane, the legendary tough cowgirl of the 1800s who lived near us in South Dakota. I listened wide-eyed to this story over and over, and each time was like the first.

It seems that Gramp, nine years old and all dressed up in short pants and a tie, was sent off to Sunday school by himself one day. Along the way, he stopped to pick up discarded whiskey bottles, then went to the town saloon to redeem them for a nickel each. Calamity Jane greeted him at the bar, took the three or four bottles he had collected, then cut off his tie with her knife and gave him a silver dollar! My great-grandparents were suspicious about this story, to say the least, but they finally decided that it was too farfetched for my grandfather to have made up.

From my perspective, silver-dollar-size pancakes are the best size to cook and to eat, especially when dipped in sugar or our famous local huckleberry honey. The little kids love to hear that story while they're downing theirs.

MAKES THIRTY 2-INCH PANCAKES

In a large bowl, combine the flour, sugar, baking powder, and salt. In a medium bowl, whisk the milk, eggs, and oil until smooth. Gradually add the milk mixture to the dry mixture, mixing with a fork until combined. Allow a few lumps. It should be the consistency of heavy cream. Add more milk or water to dilute the batter if it is too thick.

Heat a cast-iron skillet over high heat. Reduce the heat to medium and brush the skillet with butter. Drop spoonfuls of batter the size of silver dollars onto the skillet. Cook until the tops are bubbly and edges look crisp. Turn with a wide spatula and cook until golden on the underside. Transfer the pancakes to warm plates and serve immediately.

Continue making pancakes with the remaining batter, brushing the skillet with butter with each batch if necessary.

QUEEN LATIFAH
COMES HOME TO ROOST

All hail the royal poultry. And yes,
we like our green eggs and ham.
Brown ones, too.

OUR CHICKEN COOP IS REALLY A CONDO OF A HEN HOUSE WITH two separate compartments. Six Golden Sex-links live with six Barred Rocks in one unit; six exotic varieties live in the other. We do our best for our flock, providing clean water, a basic commercial feed, occasional table scraps of leftover vegetables and lettuce and oyster shells. Pecking the oyster shells provides the chickens with calorie-free calcium, which satisfies their appetites without making them too fat. In return, they all lay enormous brown eggs (the extra-large variety at the grocery store) daily. Tending to the chickens and gathering their eggs has become part of our daily routine, and a special highlight when our grandchildren are visiting.

In for a penny, in for a pound—a couple of summers ago, I decided to expand my rather pedestrian chicken collection by adding some of the so-called exotics. I began studying the chicken catalog from our local feed store, which was a much steeper learning curve than I would have imagined. A chicken, apparently, is not just a chicken, nor are all chickens created equal. I ordered a Buff Brahma Bantam, a Dark Brahma Bantam, a Silver Sebright Bantam, two Arcanas—one light and one dark—and a White Crested Black Polish. In effect, designer chickens.

While I'm sure that a trained eye can tell the differences from infancy, to those unschooled in the ways of chicks, as I am, they tend to look the same. It's only when they lose the down and acquire plumage that I can begin to declare any sort of positive identification. The most recognizable chicken from the catalog was the White Crested Black Polish, a beauty who definitely ruled the roost. We dubbed her Queen— Queen Latifah, to be exact. She had been presiding over the coop for a year when we began hearing early-morning crowing.

Right. Queen Latifah was a rooster.

FRONTIER EGGS

1 to 2 tablespoons olive oil

1/2 cup chopped onion

1 small green bell pepper, cored, seeded, and diced

1 cup diced celery

1 to 2 teaspoons chopped jalapeño chile

4 cups crushed tomatoes (canned is fine)

1 small bay leaf, crumbled

1 1/2 cups soft bread crumbs

Kosher salt and freshly ground black pepper to taste

2 cups grated cheddar cheese

8 large eggs

On the morning of Ellen's first day at the ranch, I took her down to the hen house to gather eggs. This was a bit out of Ellen's realm; reaching under a laying hen to retrieve a warm, just-laid egg was a far cry from reaching into the supermarket dairy case. I collected eggs from the nests amid squawks and clucks, then we made our exit, thanking the girls on the way out. I often prepare this dish for breakfast. It was inspired by a Creole recipe, but this frontier version is a bit less fiery.

SERVES 6 TO 8

Preheat the oven to 350°F.

Heat the oil in a large skillet over medium heat. Add the onion, bell pepper, celery, and jalapeño; cook, stirring, until softened but not browned, 4 to 5 minutes. Add the tomatoes and bay leaf; simmer until the tomatoes have cooked down and most of the water has evaporated, 20 to 30 minutes. Remove the pan from the heat and stir in the bread crumbs. Season to taste with salt and pepper.

Spread one half of the sauce on the bottom of a 9-inch square baking dish or 2-quart baking dish. Sprinkle 1 cup cheese on top. Ladle the rest of the tomato sauce over the cheese; top with the remaining 1 cup cheese. With the back of a spoon, make 8 depressions the size of an egg; crack an egg into each well.

Bake until the whites of the eggs are set and the yolks are still runny, 15 to 25 minutes (be sure to check them after 15 minutes).

PICNIC ON THE FLY

STUFFED PITA POCKETS WITH:
CURRIED CHICKEN SALAD OR
SLICED PEPPER STEAK WITH
PEPPER AND ONION MARMALADE

BROWN SUGAR–CHOCOLATE
CHIP COOKIES

CANDIED GINGER AND ORANGE PEEL

STUFFED PITA POCKETS

Flat breads with deep pockets are perfect for any picnic. When you're fishing a river and starved for more than the usual sandwich for lunch, stuffed pita is the way to go. This curried chicken salad recipe was inspired by many a good cook, including Big Timber caterer Susan Pauli and Ellen. Pepper steak and onion marmalade is another favorite. For munchies on our picnics, we store whole almonds and dried apricots in separate baggies. On the river they travel well and are nourishing, too.

CURRIED CHICKEN SALAD

SERVES 6, ENOUGH FOR 8 TO 10 PITAS

2 cups chicken stock

2 whole chicken breasts

1/2 cup mayonnaise

3 tablespoons chopped scallions, green and white parts

2 teaspoons ground cumin

1/2 teaspoon ground coriander

1/2 teaspoon turmeric

Kosher salt and freshly ground black pepper to taste

Heat the stock in a medium skillet over moderate to low heat until barely simmering. Add the chicken breasts and poach, covered, until the pink is gone from the center of the meat, 15 to 20 minutes.

Transfer the chicken to a cutting board and let cool. Discard the stock or strain and reserve for another use. When the chicken is cool enough to handle, remove the skin and bones and discard. Cut the chicken meat into 1-inch pieces. Cover and refrigerate until assembly time.

In a large bowl, combine the mayonnaise, scallions, cumin, coriander, and turmeric. Add the chicken and toss to combine. Season to taste with salt and pepper. Place in a plastic container and refrigerate until ready to use.

PEPPER STEAK WITH PEPPER AND ONION MARMALADE

Leftover pepper steak is a delicious stuffing for pitas, especially paired with this marmalade—really, a thick salsa. It can be made anytime of the year and put up in a glass jar. It gives a wonderful flavor to the meat.

Leftover Elk Pepper Steak (page 172), chilled

PEPPER AND ONION MARMALADE
MAKES 2 CUPS

2 tablespoons olive oil

3 yellow peppers, cored, seeded, and cut into 1/2-inch pieces

1 large Vidalia or other sweet onion, thinly sliced

Thinly slice the elk pepper steak and set aside.

To make the marmalade: Heat the oil in a large skillet over medium heat until it is hot but not smoking. Add the peppers and onion and reduce the heat. Cook, stirring occasionally, until the vegetables soften and come together in a thick sauce, 20 to 30 minutes. Place in a plastic container and refrigerate until ready to use.

To serve, stuff the pita with the steak slices and spread the marmalade over the steak as desired.

BROWN SUGAR-CHOCOLATE CHIP COOKIES

More brown sugar than usual makes these cookies especially crispy. This recipe has been in my file for more than twenty years. I often divide the dough in half so that I can bake now and freeze half for later. The crisp cookie is delicious anytime, but it tastes especially good on a river trip.

MAKES ABOUT 2 DOZEN 3-INCH COOKIES

1 cup (2 sticks) unsalted butter

1½ cups firmly packed brown sugar

½ cup granulated sugar

2 large eggs

1¾ cups sifted all-purpose flour

½ teaspoon baking soda

½ teaspoon kosher salt

1 teaspoon pure vanilla extract

1 cup (one 6-ounce package) semisweet chocolate chips

Preheat the oven to 375°F. Grease a large baking sheet.

In a large mixing bowl with an electric mixer on high, cream the butter, brown sugar, and granulated sugar until light and fluffy, 3 to 4 minutes. Add the eggs one at a time and beat well.

In a medium bowl, combine the sifted flour, baking soda, and salt. Add to the butter mixture and beat on low speed until fully incorporated. With a wooden spoon, fold in the vanilla and chocolate.

Drop the dough by tablespoons, 2 inches apart, onto the prepared baking sheet. Bake for about 7 minutes for soft and chewy cookies, about 9 minutes for crispy cookies.

CANDIED GINGER AND ORANGE PEEL

If you want to get gold stars, make this candied peel. It takes some doing—three days, cooking on and off to let the candy steep—but it's worth every minute to have a homemade version of something this good. It keeps in an airtight container for a couple of months at room temperature.

MAKES ABOUT 1 POUND

4 thick-skinned navel oranges

8 ounces fresh ginger
(2 to 3 branches), peeled
and sliced (not too thin)

6 1/2 cups sugar

6 cups water

Quarter the oranges lengthwise and remove the peel, inlcuding the white part. (Reserve the fruit for another use.) Cut the peel into 1/2-inch-wide strips. Soak the peel in cold water for 1 hour. Drain.

Transfer the peel to a 6-quart heavy pot and add cold water to cover by 1 inch. Bring to a boil, reduce the heat, and simmer 10 minutes; drain.

Add the ginger to the orange peel and repeat the blanching process 2 times. Drain the peel and ginger and set aside.

Combine 6 cups sugar and the water in the emptied pot. Bring to a boil, stirring until the sugar is dissolved. Wash down any sugar crystals clinging to the side of the pot with a pastry brush dipped in cold water. Boil the syrup, uncovered, until it registers 220°F on a candy thermometer, about 30 minutes. Add the peel and ginger and simmer over low heat until translucent, about 45 minutes. Remove from the heat and let the peel and ginger stand in the syrup, uncovered, at room temperature overnight.

The next day, return the syrup with the peel and ginger to a boil; boil, uncovered, until it registers 228°F on the thermometer, about 30 minutes. Remove from the heat and let the peel and ginger stand in the syrup, uncovered, at room temperature overnight.

The next day, reheat the syrup with the peel and ginger over low heat just until the syrup has liquefied. Drain the ginger and the peel in a colander. (Reserve the syrup for another use or discard.) Spread the peel and ginger pieces, separating them, on metal racks to dry, uncovered, until slightly tacky, overnight.

The next day, spread the remaining 1/2 cup sugar on a plate. Dredge each piece of peel and ginger in the sugar to coat well. Transfer to waxed paper and dry for 1 hour. Store in tins in layers separated by waxed paper.

The code of the West Boulder Reserve is Keep 'em Swimming.

HUCKLEBERRIES AND FINS

TROUT FISHING IN AMERICA IS NOW RULED BY AN UNWRITTEN law: catch and release. Dedicated anglers, especially fly fishermen, get their biggest kicks these days hooking a wild trout and then throwing it back into the stream. The trout-depleted streams are replenishing themselves, and the most avid trout fishermen are more pleased about this than anyone else.

Even so, catch and release is not a hard-and-fast rule when you're in Montana's backcountry, on a long trip with an unappetizing assortment of freeze-dried vacuum-sealed backpacking meals. A fresh trout taken from the newly bountiful streams of the wilderness is a delicacy to be savored without guilt or recrimination.

One of America's greatest fly fishermen and dedicated conservationists is our friend Yvon Chouinard, a marketing genius who created the clothing and outdoor-gear company Patagonia. Yvon cherishes the chance to test himself and his friends against the demands of wild places, climbing rock walls and frozen waterfalls. But he also believes in the rewards of a memorable meal in those remote settings where the supermarket is fifty miles away and a long, hard hike over the mountains. He didn't just create Patagonia; he lives it.

A few years ago seven of us, adults and kids, all backpacked into the vast Bob Marshall Wilderness of Montana for a trip meant to last four days. We were expecting to see glorious vistas, alpine lakes and streams, magnificent peaks with huge waterfalls, meadows showcasing many varieties of wildflowers, and possibly signs of grizzly bears. I say signs of grizzlies because unless the bears were so far away that we needed binoculars to get a good look, we weren't looking for close encounters. These bears can be dangerous.

On this trip Tom and I did experience an unusual sight of another sort. We were sound asleep in our sleeping bags when the shaking ground woke us both. It wasn't an earthquake but rather the Sun River elk herd, about three hundred strong, crossing the stream right in front of our tent in the predawn. They were practically right on top of us; we could see their huge brown bodies through the transparent flap of our tent. It was thrilling.

We had the usual assortment of carry-along and freeze-dried food with us. The schedule was to hike all day, set up camp late in the afternoon, and boil water from a nearby stream in order to rehydrate the freeze-dried food. On about day three, when the packets of dried stroganoff and instant rice were beginning to lose their appeal, Yvon saved the day. The fishermen among us assembled their backpack fly rods and headed for the river. We had spotted some watercress growing wild by the stream and huckleberry bushes filled with ripe berries, so while they were fishing, a couple of us began gathering our salad and dessert.

The fishing expedition was successful, and we had two beautiful rainbows to wrap in foil and cook over the coals. One of the fish, a female, provided roe for an additional treat. The meal consisted of trout, watercress salad tossed with olive oil, and flat bread baked on top of hot rocks. Our inventive friend Yvon had brought a small bag of flour and sourdough starter, which he kept warm at night in a Ziploc bag in the bottom of his sleeping bag. Never had food tasted better.

This was a four-star meal under the stars.

Every fisherman knows there are cutthroats, rainbows, and brownies lurking below the ripples in these teeming waters.

IT'S A CUTTHROAT LIFE

BY JAMES PROSEK

AS A CONNECTICUT YANKEE, IT'S ALWAYS A treat to go out West in summer, in particular to northwest Wyoming–southwest Montana. Things aren't as green and enclosed there as they are at home. A whole new palette takes over—ochers, umber, sienna, naples yellow—and an entire spectrum of blues that just don't exist in the East. From the point of view of someone who loves to paint in watercolors, it's a highly nuanced and very exciting landscape to be in and to savor. The observant angler soon notices that the entire landscape of colors—crimsons and sunset oranges of the evening sky, the cadmium and viridian greens of the evergreens, the softness of morning light on a yellowing field of grass—can also be seen in the coloration of the native cutthroat trout.

I welcomed the opportunity to visit Meredith and Tom and stay at their ranch, to fish the river and to paint. I came to Livingston and stayed in the Murray Hotel for a few days to acclimatize myself to western life. I browsed books at Sax and Fryer Bookstore and had a drink with John Fryer at the Owl Bar. "Livingston will never become as commercial as Bozeman," he said. "The dirt's too thin and the wind blows too hard."

With the Yellowstone River on its doorstep, Livingston is a great town for someone who loves trout. All the heroes of fly-fishing have passed through or gotten stuck here at one time or another. So it was especially amazing to follow the directions to the West Boulder Ranch and discover a secluded nook that I would never have imagined was there, and to see the beautiful river snaking quietly through. Here, not far from its source in the Absaroka Wilderness, the West Boulder wound around big boulders (hence the name) covered with soft green and orange lichen and over colorful gravel. It was so unusual, so unlike other rivers I'd fished in North America; it reminded me most of a stream I'd fished in northern Portugal. I couldn't wait to fish it.

The water was low, as it usually is that time of year, and fires were burning to the west, but Tom said the fishing had been good. We headed out with our fly rods the next morning with Sage, a yellow Lab, and Abbie, a black Lab, fishing alongside us. Tom and I took turns casting in each pool; the scale of the pools is too intimate to be fished by more than one angler at a time. The boulders in the river provided good cover for us as we stalked the fish. And as long as we made a good cast we were certain to have a trout, if not take the fly, at least inspect it. The trout are mostly cutthroat (usually hybridized with the rainbows).

The next afternoon Tom and I fished upstream of the house and the stables, where the river wound sharply through the meadows. I fished on up ahead for a while and watched a coyote stalking several geese. Then Tom called me back to where he was to see what he'd found. At the bottom of the stream, by his feet, was a cutthroat trout about ten inches long that had a garter snake about two and a half feet long hanging out of its mouth. We stood there for some time, looking at the trout with the partially digested snake in its gut. I think Tom shared my feeling that somehow it was a significant sight. It was odd to see nature, which we always hear is in "balance," overextend itself. We puzzled out what had probably happened. The snake had begun crossing the river when the trout came up and grabbed it by the head. But it was too big to swallow, and in the ensuing struggle, both the snake and the trout died. I've played out the scene in my mind many times since. Was it an allegory of greed and its consequences? By the time we got back to the ranch, Tom and I had honed our story of the trout and the snake so that we could give Meredith a concise report from the field. We referred to the trout as the "ambitious fish."

The predator-prey relationship was not always a simple equation (though we were pretty sure that there was no trout large enough to swallow us headfirst while crossing the West Boulder River). As anglers, out on the stream all day, we were predators, too. We stalked trout and cast imitations of insects in the hope of hooking one. These days, we let most of the fish go. But Tom believed, as I did, that it was necessary to kill and eat the occasional trout to remind ourselves that we fish because of an evolutionary urge.

One afternoon he said, "Let's get a trout for dinner."

Three years earlier, he had stocked some pure-strain Westslope Cutthroat trout in a pond on the property.

"This spring," he told me, "I went out in a canoe and saw these huge fish. I went to the head cowboy, David, and I said, 'Geez, David, how did those big carp get in our pond?'

"'Those ain't carp,' David said."

Tom ran back to the house to grab his fly rod and cast out a big woolly bugger. On the first cast he hooked and landed a six-pound cutthroat, a fish many would consider historic in size.

We arrived at the pond in the late afternoon. It was broad and shallow, with twisted stumps of old trees and mats of thick green weed. We saw some fish move, making a wake like a shoal of tarpon. I cast once, began to retrieve the fly, and saw a wake so big that I pulled the fly away in fright. I cast again and hooked one.

"It's huge, huge!" I yelled. It was twenty-three inches long, a gorgeous fish: orange like squash blossoms, with scarlet and yellow on the gill plates, copper-and-Tuscan-red fins, and a broad tail like an open hand covered with coal-black specks. I was very excited. Tom was equally proud of his fish.

"Now you can tell your friends that the most beautiful trout you ever caught was on the West Boulder Ranch," Tom said.

That was not a stretch at all. And though it was beautiful alive, it was also satisfying to know that it would be beautiful on a platter with fresh herbs.

That evening we brushed the trout with olive oil and lemon juice; stuffed the cavity with butter, rosemary, and parsley; wrapped it in tinfoil; and cooked it on the charcoal grill. We ate it with fresh vegetables from Meredith's garden, and it was darn good.

COW CAMP LUNCH

LEMONADE SANGRIA

PERFECT BISON BURGERS

GRANDMA JEAN'S EASY
BREAD-AND-BUTTER PICKLES

ROCKY MOUNTAIN POTATO SALAD

CILANTRO SLAW

WATERMELON AND FETA SALAD

FUDGY BROWNIES

CHOWING DOWN AT COW CAMP:
*There's no such thing as too much
food here. Everything gets eaten.
Everything but the wildflowers,
that is. (At right, a single stem of
purple horse mint.)*

LEMONADE SANGRIA

Lemonade for a picnic can be refreshing and zesty if you garnish it with berries, fruit slices, and mint to zip up the taste. Sangria typically is wine with fruit, but the idea is the same.

SERVES 6 TO 8

5 lemons (about 1 pound)

2 quarts water

3 to 4 tablespoons sugar to taste

1 cup blueberries, raspberries, peach slices, or fruit of your choice

18 fresh mint leaves

Squeeze the juice of the lemons into the water (you should have about 1 cup juice). Add the sugar to taste. Pour the sangria into each glass and garnish with berries or fruit slices of your choice and a few mint leaves.

PERFECT BISON BURGERS

There are two tricks to making a good burger: don't overhandle the meat, and don't overcook it, especially if it's bison. Bison meat is very lean—almost no fat—so it tends to overcook easily. It's better for our health because of the lack of animal fat, but it requires understanding.

The fixings can also make or break a good hamburger. The buns need to be buttered lightly and toasted or grilled. Crispy lettuce, slices of ripe tomato, and slices of red or sweet onion are all the necessary partners for the burger's perfection. Our McLeod Hot Mustard is a good addition, and ketchup is a must.

SERVES 6

3 pounds ground bison (see Selected Sources) or beef

1/4 cup (1/2 stick) butter, softened

6 hamburger buns (sesame seed, poppy seed, onion, or plain)

6 iceberg lettuce leaves, washed and dried

6 slices ripe tomato

6 slices onion (red, Vidalia, or Walla Walla)

Ketchup

McLeod Hot Mustard (page 198)

Mayonnaise (optional)

Prepare a hot grill.

Form the meat into 6 patties, being careful not to overhandle. Place the patties on the grill rack 3 to 4 inches over direct heat and grill, turning once, about 2 minutes per side for medium/rare.

Spread each bun half with 1 teaspoon butter. Place the buns, buttered sides down, on the grill rack and toast briefly.

Assemble the burgers with the toasted buns, patties, lettuce, tomato slices, onion slices, ketchup, mustard, and mayonnaise (if using).

Hardy mountain wildflowers—lupine, Queen Anne's lace, horse mint, daisies, geraniums, sego lilies, and blue bells—are all the decoration my picnic table needs.

WHERE THE WOOLLY MAMMOTH ROAMED

I FEEL ECHOES OF HISTORY EVERYWHERE IN MONTANA, BUT THE past never feels closer than on the ride to Cow Camp, an old log cabin nestled in a basin about two miles from the ranch over rugged and seemingly untouched land.

A friend and neighbor, the archaeologist Dr. Larry Lahren, describes in detail the world of the first hunter-gatherers in this draw, for whom the topography, and possibly much of the flora and fauna, looked just as they do today. Arriving shortly after the last glaciers left the area about eleven thousand years ago, these inhabitants hunted lions, cheetahs, caribou, woolly mammoths, and giant sloths along with the elk, bison, deer, and moose we find today.

More recent people who claimed this land during the last millennium have left extensive evidence of their way of life. Dr. Lahren has combed the area and found teepee rings—circles that mark campsites—huge boulders used for hunting blinds, gravesites, arrowheads, stone tools, and a buffalo jump where the animals were slaughtered, skinned, and prepared for food.

Most people are seduced by the expansive vistas, the flowers growing wild, and the glimpses of the animals, which perhaps own this land most of all. Not Dr. Lahren. What he sees, for example, is a dim but distinct trail left by a travois, the hand-pulled cart used by the Crow, the Sheepeaters, and the Shoshones, all of whom were earlier inhabitants of the area. He describes their way of life, what they ate, where they traveled, and how they used the land. Before long, you feel the presence of these ancient peoples who watched the same sun rise and fall over these majestic mountains.

Now fast-forward to Cow Camp. It's been called that—or the line shack—for almost a century, though our old-timers can't quite come up with the origins of the name. It possibly started out as a homestead; it has definitely housed many sheepherders, cowboys, and hunters over the years. Two miles from home may not seem like much, but those two hours up and ninety minutes down means that you don't go when time is an issue. Most guests at the ranch ride or hike up to Cow Camp at least once during their visit; it's far enough away to seem remote but close enough to be accessible. The panoramic view of the mountains is breathtaking, still unmarred by "progress." The alpine wildflowers— sego lilies, wild iris, bluebells, Indian paintbrush—are everywhere. More often than not, we spot elk, antelope, or black bears, and sometimes all of them, on our trips. The raptor population—red-tailed hawks, marsh hawks, golden and bald eagles, as well as many different kinds of owls— is also abundant.

Nature throws us some curves as well, as if to remind us of its dominance. The sharp clatter of a diamondback rattlesnake's warning is a familiar sound, and always unsettling. The horses spend every night out in the pastures and certainly come upon rattlesnakes in their travels. Even though none has ever been bitten, it's not unheard of. Because of this, during hot spells, I've learned it's preferable to ride in early morning or late in the day.

And now there are wolves. One of the most hotly debated and controversial subjects in the West has been the reintroduction of the North American wolf into Yellowstone Park. This powerful canine was central to the ecosystem before being eradicated in the last century by

hunters and ranchers who failed to appreciate anything about the animal. Now that the wolves are back, the dynamics of Yellowstone and the surrounding territory have changed, and wolf biologists are doing their best to track their numbers and calibrate their impact on the environment. Elk are the primary food source for wolves in these parts, but human beings hunting around the park would prefer not to share the quarry with them. Ranchers likewise are concerned about wolf impact on their sheep and cattle. Fortunately, not much livestock has been lost, and where wolves have killed sheep and cattle the ranchers have been reimbursed by the government for their losses. It's unusual to spot the shy wolves on this ride, although sharp eyes have seen their tracks all around the camp.

The cabin at Cow Camp has a Coleman stove and small bottles of propane. A metal trunk is stocked with dishes and utensils and such other essentials as salt and pepper, so that the saddlebags on the horses need carry only items for the picnic once we've arrived. (All leftovers and trash get packed the same way for the trip back down.) There's a well-used wood-burning stove as well, a set of bunk beds, a kitchen table, and several handmade wooden chairs.

History, nature, and ecology aside, a group of my women neighbors—Julie, Laurie, and Nan—ride up to Cow Camp and spend one night there every summer. We've dubbed ourselves the Whistle Creek Women, and we enjoy hiking and riding together all season, but the overnight is a cherished tradition. We've had great adventures together over the years; twice we've paddled in canoes, camping along the way down a wilderness section of the Missouri River well known as a site of Lewis and Clark camps during their 1804 journey. We keep the food simple—usually a steak with stir-fry vegetables—so that we can get on with our poker game. We light a fire in the old wood stove, sit around the slightly rickety kitchen table, and deal. The stakes aren't high. When we're done, we put a few rolls of nickels on a wooden shelf inside the front door and leave them behind for next year's game. Even so, this is serious business. Future archaeologists, take note.

RIDING HIGH: *Andie Brokaw Simon with her husband, Charles, framed by the Beartooth Absaroka range (opposite).* LILY OF OUR VALLEY: *The sego lily is actually the state flower of Utah, but it's a beautiful addition to any Montana bouquet (below).*

GRANDMA JEAN'S EASY
BREAD-AND-BUTTER PICKLES

5 small Kirby cucumbers,
sliced into 1-inch-thick
rounds

1 cup sliced white onion

2 cups sugar

1 cup cider vinegar

1 tablespoon celery seed

1 tablespoon mustard seed

1 tablespoon pickling salt

This recipe is from Tom's mother, Jean, who's still going strong and is as sharp as a tack. Nothing gets past her; she raised three great sons, and she doesn't miss a trick. These pickles are the easy ones in her cooking file, although she's even better known for her canned dills. She told Ellen how she used to make gallons of them when friends brought the good-size cucumbers to her. Gallons, mind you, and those pickles were canned—and they were much more complicated to put up than these bread-and-butter ones. The truth is, she could hardly keep up with the demand for pickles, in any form, from her husband, Red, and the three boys—Tom, Bill, and Mike.

MAKES THREE TO FOUR 8-OUNCE JARS

In a large bowl, combine the cucumbers, onion, sugar, vinegar, celery seed, mustard seed, and pickling salt. Transfer to 8-ounce Mason jars or other jars with tight-fitting lids. Refrigerate for 2 to 3 days before serving. The pickles will keep for up to 2 weeks—if they last that long.

ROCKY MOUNTAIN POTATO SALAD

16 to 18 medium new potatoes,
or 26 to 30 small new potatoes

1/2 cup chopped celery

1/3 cup chopped scallions,
white and green parts

1/2 jalapeño chile, seeded and
diced fine (optional)

1/2 cup mayonnaise

1/2 cup sour cream

2 tablespoons prepared mustard

1 tablespoon red wine vinegar

2 teaspoons kosher salt

1 teaspoon coarsely ground
black pepper

Tabasco sauce to taste

This recipe stands out because of the crunch of celery and scallions and the zap of jalapeño pepper. We store it in a cooler and usually transport it by truck on the ride to Cow Camp, and it travels well that way. At home we like to serve it slightly warm, but on a long ride we need to keep it cool.

SERVES 6 TO 8

Combine the potatoes with enough water to cover and a pinch of salt in a large saucepan. Bring to a boil over high heat. Reduce the heat and simmer until tender when pierced with a sharp knife, 30 to 40 minutes. Drain and quarter the potatoes; place in a bowl.

Add the celery, scallions, japapeño (if using), mayonnaise, sour cream, mustard, vinegar, salt, and pepper. Add a dash or two of Tabasco sauce, or more if you like. Serve the salad warm or at room temperature. Or cover and refrigerate and serve chilled.

CILANTRO SLAW

This slaw features aromatic cilantro, a fresh herb that grows well in our garden. Coriander and Chinese parsley are other names for this leaf, which originated in the Caribbean and Mexico and is widely used in India and the Far East as well. It's nice to know that an herb can bring the world together in a single dish. What we like about this salad is its fresh, clean taste and that wonderful scent. Make it the day you intend to serve it so that it's really crisp.

SERVES 6 TO 8

1 medium head white cabbage, finely shredded

1 small onion, minced

1/2 cup chopped fresh cilantro leaves

1 cucumber, peeled, seeded, and chopped

3/4 cup olive oil

1/4 cup freshly squeezed lime juice

2 medium garlic cloves, minced

Kosher salt and freshly ground black pepper to taste

In a large bowl or salad bowl, mix together the cabbage and onion. Add the cilantro and cucumber and toss lightly. Cover with plastic wrap or a clean dishtowel and refrigerate.

In a small bowl, whisk together the olive oil, lime juice, garlic, salt, and pepper. Set aside.

About 1 hour before serving, pour half the dressing onto the slaw and toss lightly. Refrigerate until serving time. Use the remaining dressing for salads or grilled vegetables.

WATERMELON AND FETA SALAD

In Big Timber, a town of seventeen hundred people just northeast of us, lives Susan Pauli, a great gal and wonderful cook who is in great demand as a caterer. She makes this unusual summer creation as soon as the local watermelons have ripened. The pink color is gorgeous, and the salad travels well. Who would have thought that feta cheese and black pepper together would enhance the taste of watermelon?

PHOTOGRAPH ON PAGE 65

SERVES 6 TO 8

3 cups 2-inch chunks watermelon, seeded

1 cup crumbled feta cheese

Coarsely ground black pepper to taste

1/2 teaspoon red pepper flakes (optional)

In a large bowl, combine the watermelon, feta, and a few generous grindings of black pepper. For a little more zing, add the red pepper flakes, if you like. Serve immediately.

FUDGY BROWNIES

There are two camps of people in the brownie competition: the cake people and the fudge people. The cake people like theirs with an extra egg, and the fudgers like theirs sticky, like candy. The secret to having fudgy brownies is to slightly undercook them.

MAKES TWELVE 2-INCH SQUARES

1 cup (2 sticks) unsalted butter, plus more for greasing the pan

1½ cups (9 ounces) semisweet chocolate chips

3 ounces unsweetened chocolate, chopped

1 cup sugar

3 large eggs

1 tablespoon pure vanilla extract

1 cup all-purpose flour, plus more for flouring the pan

1½ teaspoons baking powder

Pinch of kosher salt

Preheat the oven to 350°F. Butter and flour the bottom of an 8-inch square glass baking dish. Knock out any excess flour.

In a glass measuring cup, combine the butter, chocolate chips, and unsweetened chocolate; microwave on high until melted, 30 to 40 seconds.

In a medium bowl, combine the melted chocolate, sugar, eggs, and vanilla. Cool slightly.

In a large bowl, combine the flour, baking powder, and salt. Add the chocolate mixture and beat by hand with a spoon for 40 strokes. Scrape the batter into the prepared pan. Bake for 40 to 50 minutes. Check for doneness by inserting a toothpick in the center of the brownies. If it comes out clean, it's too done. If it shows some chocolate batter, but not too much, it's perfect. The center will set as it cools.

"WHOA"—CHILI BREAK

SPINACH SALAD WITH BACON TWISTS

GORGONZOLA CROUTONS

JALAPEÑO CORN BREAD

CHICKEN CHILI

SPICY SALSA

CHOCOLATE BUTTERMILK CUPCAKES

SPINACH SALAD WITH BACON TWISTS

Finding crispy crumbled bacon in a spinach salad is not unusual, but these long twists set this one apart in the looks department. Our garden-grown spinach is always fresh and so full of healthy nutrients. Add the blue cheese croutons and garnish with hard-boiled eggs for a more complete dish.

SERVES 6 TO 8

6 to 8 strips uncooked bacon

2 garlic cloves, minced

1/4 cup olive oil

3 tablespoons mayonnaise

1 tablespoon red wine vinegar

2 teaspoons honey

1 pound spinach, tough stems removed, washed well, and spun dry

1/2 red onion, thinly sliced

Gorgonzola Croutons (recipe follows)

2 hard-boiled eggs, peeled and halved or quartered (optional)

Preheat the oven to 375°F.

Arrange the bacon slices on a rack over a broiler pan, twisting each slice and pressing the ends down to hold the twist in place. Bake in the center of the oven until very crisp, about 15 minutes. They may unravel a bit, but don't worry. Transfer the twists to paper towels to drain.

To make the dressing, combine the garlic, olive oil, mayonnaise, vinegar, and honey in a jar and shake well; set aside.

Place the spinach and onion in a salad bowl. Add the dressing and toss well to coat. Top the salad with the bacon twists, croutons, and hard-cooked eggs, if you like.

GORGONZOLA CROUTONS

2 tablespoons crumbled Gorgonzola cheese

2 teaspoons butter, at room temperature

2 (1/2-inch-thick) slices sourdough or Tuscan peasant bread

Preheat the oven to 375°F.

Mash the cheese and butter together and spread on the bread; place on a baking sheet. Bake until the bread is toasted and the topping is bubbly, about 15 minutes. You can bake the croutons in the oven along with the bacon.

Let cool. Cut into squares.

Spinach Salad with Bacon Twists along with Jalapeño Corn Bread (page 70)

JALAPEÑO CORN BREAD

1 cup yellow cornmeal

1 cup all-purpose flour

¼ cup sugar

1 tablespoon baking powder

Pinch of kosher salt

3 large eggs

1 cup heavy cream

¼ cup (½ stick) butter, melted

1 cup fresh or frozen corn kernels

⅓ cup grated sharp white cheddar cheese

1 small jalapeño pepper, seeded and finely chopped (see Note)

This recipe of Ellen's was inspired by a dear friend and a good judge of food. We've added a hint of a spicy jalapeño pepper to supply some zest, especially for our western neighbors. Wrap it in aluminum foil for a river trip or a ride; you can count on having only crumbs at the end of the day.

PHOTOGRAPH ON PAGE 69

SERVES 8

Preheat the oven to 375°F. Butter an 8-inch square baking dish.

In a large mixing bowl, combine the cornmeal, flour, sugar, baking powder, and salt; mix with a fork. Stir in the eggs, cream, and melted butter. Fold in the corn, cheese, and jalapeño pepper until well distributed.

Spoon the batter into the prepared baking dish. Bake until a cake tester or toothpick inserted in the center of the corn bread comes out clean, 30 to 35 minutes.

NOTE: Fresh jalapeño peppers vary in their bite. The fat larger ones seem to be milder than the small ones, but this is not a hard-and-fast rule, only an observation. Always check for yourself.

CHICKEN CHILI

People have strong opinions about chili. I've heard grown men argue about the merits of chili with beans. "What? Never had chili with beans! That isn't even chili!" After a hard day's work, it scarcely matters which kind it is, because people are hungry, period. This recipe for white chili is ever-so-good. It was concocted by our ranch manager, Karen Campbell. It's different—and something to talk about.

SERVES 6 TO 8

1 tablespoon olive oil

1/4 cup chopped onion

1 cup chicken broth (canned is fine)

1/2 cup Spicy Salsa (recipe follows) or 1/2 cup canned diced tomatoes and green chiles

1 (4-ounce) can green chiles, drained and chopped

2 pounds grilled chicken meat, cut into bite-size strips

2 tablespoons chopped fresh cilantro

2 teaspoons chopped fresh oregano, or 1 teaspoon dried

2 teaspoons ground cumin

1 teaspoon garlic powder

1/8 teaspoon cayenne pepper

1 (15.5-ounce) can cannellini beans, drained

12 flour tortillas

6 tablespoons butter, softened

Sour cream, salsa, grated Jack cheese, and chopped Vidalia onions or scallions

In a large saucepan, heat the olive oil over moderate heat until hot but not smoking. Add the onion and cook, stirring, until opaque, 2 to 3 minutes.

Stir in the broth, salsa or tomatoes, chiles, chicken, cilantro, oregano, cumin, garlic powder, and cayenne. Simmer for 20 minutes. Add the beans and cook, stirring occasionally, until the sauce thickens, about 20 minutes longer.

Preheat the oven to 200°F for soft tortillas, or 300°F for crispy tortillas.

For soft tortillas: Butter each tortilla lightly, stack them, and wrap in aluminum foil. Warm in the oven for 10 minutes.

For crispy baked tortillas: Omit the butter. Cut the tortillas into triangles and spray or brush with vegetable oil. Place them on baking sheets and bake until crisp, about 30 minutes.

Serve the chili with sour cream, additional salsa, Jack cheese, chopped onions or scallions, and the tortillas.

SPICY SALSA

3/4 cup diced tomatoes

1 tablespoon finely chopped jalapeño pepper

2 tablespoons canned chopped green chiles

1 teaspoon paprika

1 teaspoon Worcestershire sauce

1 teaspoon kosher salt

Freshly ground black pepper to taste

This easy salsa is great to have on hand, especially for hardy spice lovers to add to their chili.

MAKES 1 CUP

Toss together all the ingredients and serve.

CHOCOLATE BUTTERMILK CUPCAKES

2½ cups cake flour

½ cup unsweetened cocoa powder

2 teaspoons baking soda
   Pinch of kosher salt

1 cup (2 sticks) unsalted butter, softened

2¼ cups sugar

2 large eggs

2 cups buttermilk

1 teaspoon pure vanilla extract

CHOCOLATE FROSTING

6 ounces unsweetened chocolate, finely chopped

½ cup (1 stick) unsalted butter, softened

1 tablespoon pure vanilla extract

1½ cups sugar

1 cup heavy cream

Light, fluffy, chocolaty, and unbelievably delicious: That pretty much sums up these cupcakes. My grandmother used to make them, and they've made their way into all of our families' kitchens.

MAKES 24 CUPCAKES

Preheat the oven to 350°F. Butter and flour 24 muffin-pan cups or insert paper cupcake liners.

In a medium bowl, combine the flour, cocoa, baking soda, and salt. In a large bowl using an electric mixer on medium speed, cream the butter, sugar, and eggs until light and fluffy. Add the buttermilk and vanilla and beat on low speed. Spoon in the flour mixture little by little and mix until well combined.

Spoon the batter into the muffin cups. Bake until a cake tester or toothpick inserted in the center of the cupcakes comes out clean, about 20 minutes. Cool completely before frosting.

To make the frosting: In a medium bowl, combine the chocolate, butter, and vanilla; stir until smooth, about 30 seconds. In a heavy saucepan over medium-high heat, bring the sugar and cream to a boil. Lower the heat and cook, stirring, until the sugar dissolves. Reduce the heat and simmer, stirring often, for 5 minutes.

Remove the pan from the heat and stir in the chocolate mixture. Cover and refrigerate for at least 1 hour.

To frost the cupcakes: Remove the frosting from the refrigerator and beat it to make it soft enough to spread.

TAKING STOCK

BY TOM McGUANE

THE ENCHANTMENT OF RIDING IS A MYSTERIOUS thing that generates never-ending reflection for those who wish to understand the mild euphoria produced by the proximity of horses. This is not the province of equestrian recreationists alone; the evidence abounds that Native Americans, cavalrymen, cowboys, and farmers were vulnerable to this sweeping affection, which finds itself in close bonds on the one hand and insatiable accumulation on the other. Among the accumulators are buffalo-hunting Indians, Coca-Cola heirs, sheiks, oilmen, and soon-to-be-bankrupt professors. The Plains Indians were liberated from the midwestern forests by the horse, and the cruelest strikes against their civilization were the execution of their horses, as at the Sand Creek Massacre, where a Methodist minister named Carrington tried to put a whole people afoot by killing their mounts.

That my house adjoins my corrals is one of the blessings of my adult life. I start very few days without taking my coffee out to stand among our horses so that we may contemplate the beginning of another day. When I'm stressful or troubled that I can't make a piece of work come out right, or a friend or family member has received unsettling health news, or some other unhappy or unpleasant feeling comes over me that won't find a quiet place of storage, a visit to the horses nearly always produces relief. Relief and perspective, which is perhaps the same thing.

When we had an irrevocably dying horse, my veterinarian told me that we had to change our perspective and try to understand that animals accept what happens to them. And it's not that they don't know. They know. We humans, on the other hand, have evolved to accept nothing. We don't accept how fast we go, how long we live, how much we eat, how frequently we copulate. Our position is: *It's all negotiable* or *I'll buy my way out of this*. In the life of horses, grave things happen from birth to death and they never negotiate; their bank accounts contain only the memories of their race.

Back to my corrals: The gates to native grass pastures are seldom closed, but there they are to see us anyway. We've swindled them with treats but are flattered because they seem glad to see us, and affection must be dealt evenhandedly to avoid jealousy. The personalities are very distinct: the erratic yearlings striving, not always successfully, for acceptance; the old mare with the frozen ears who requires twice the space the others need; a daydreaming mother-to-be, the star cutting horse who declared at twelve, by refusing ever to get into a trailer again, that her days of competition were over; the foursquare and uncomplicatedly heroic cow horse who shambles around like Ollie the Dragon but breathes fire when working cattle; my wife's cutting horse, informal inspector of all ranch activities; my head-case saddle horse, who spooks at grasshoppers; the trusting young mare who among all our horses is alone allowed to transport the grandchildren; the tall bay mare, the stately mother of champions—and I'm afraid what some would say are too many others. The largest group is the pensioners, aged ranch horses living serenely in a riparian cottonwood forest; and, beyond, the burial ground where our old mounts, old friends, lie—most at the end of long lives but some that were too short: a fall that broke a neck, a lightning strike, a twisted gut.

In 1957, I loped across a Wyoming pasture trying to rope a calf. After three unsuccessful throws, my horse stopped suddenly on his front feet and I sailed onto the ground in front of him, useless lariat in hand. To this day, I remember the contemplative look on that horse's face as he gazed at me on the ground, and the quiet acceptance as he let me climb on again. We'd agreed to accept my limitations, and to jog on home together. It's unique to share a time, to share a job, with a partner who doesn't judge you, even over the span of years. It occurs to you that you might do the same. Long exposure to horses should teach tolerance. One accomplished equestrian said you'll never be a champion until you understand and accept the limitations of each horse. Certainly horses accept that humans can't see very far, smell very much, or hear very well. Our lurching two-legged slowness must seem amusing to any horse that doesn't wish to be caught. Every day, a rider must be reminded by his horse how little he notices about the surface of the earth. Squirrelly as we are, horses tolerate us and our addled, sex-crazed, money-grubbing, vengeful brains.

Apparently there are more and more horses, more than ever before, shaded up, switching flies, traveling in single file to water, bucking off cowboys, leading parades, amusing children, skidding logs, sorting cattle, climbing mountains, carrying supplies—another society, almost, invading human loneliness.

CAMP RUNAMUCK SNACK

STETSON SALAD

SPICY TOMATO SOUP

TOASTED PARSLEYED PITA CRISPS

STRAWBERRY FOOL

ICEBOX SUGAR COOKIES

STETSON SALAD

This is a dish that can meet the needs of a few people or a crowd. It's named after a pottery company called Stetson and has nothing to do with the cowboy hat, although it does look like a Western wagon wheel. The salad is served on a round plate of wedge-shape sections filled with healthy ingredients such as shredded chicken, spinach, roasted corn, cheese, and currants, topped off with an aïoli and pesto dressing. All in all, it's an unusual salad, and a winner. One of the ingredients, quinoa, pronounced "keen-wah," is a grain native to South America, related to spinach and Swiss chard. It's high in nutrients, especially iron and protein.

SERVES 8 TO 10

4 cups cooked quinoa
  (from 2 cups uncooked)

2 cups shredded cooked
  chicken breast

2 cups dried roasted corn
  (such as JustCorn; see
  Selected Sources)

1 cup grated Asiago cheese

1 cup salted roasted pumpkin
  seeds

1 cup dried currants

1½ cups chopped tomatoes

2 cups chopped spinach or
  arugula

STETSON DRESSING

2 small shallots, diced

1 cup buttermilk

1 cup Easy Aïoli (recipe follows)

½ cup pesto, store-bought or
  homemade (recipe follows)

2 tablespoons freshly
  squeezed lemon juice

½ teaspoon freshly ground
  black pepper

Make a bed of quinoa on a large round shallow serving plate. Arrange the chicken, corn, cheese, pumpkin seeds, currants, tomatoes, and spinach on top of the quinoa in 7 wedge-shape sections.

To make the dressing: In a medium bowl, combine the shallots, buttermilk, aïoli, pesto, lemon juice, and pepper. You will have approximately 3 cups.

Serve the dressing in a pitcher for your guests to drizzle on their salad. Reserve the remaining dressing in a glass jar, refrigerated, for other salads.

EASY AÏOLI

MAKES ABOUT 1 CUP

¾ cup olive oil

¼ cup chopped garlic

1 teaspoon kosher salt

Combine the olive oil, garlic, and salt in a small bowl. Refrigerate, covered, for up to 1 week.

PESTO

MAKES ABOUT ¾ CUP

½ cup olive oil

¼ cup fresh basil leaves

1 tablespoon pine nuts

1 teaspoon kosher salt

In the bowl of a food processor, pulse the olive oil, basil, pine nuts, and salt until combined. Refrigerate, covered, for 2 or 3 days.

SPICY TOMATO SOUP

We serve this soup in little mugs at our family reunions. With a choice of garnishes—lemon slices, chopped fresh herbs or scallion greens, or even toasted pine nuts—our guests can suit themselves.

SERVES 6 TO 8

4 teaspoons olive oil

6 medium garlic cloves, minced

1 tablespoon paprika

2 teaspoons ground cumin

$1/2$ teaspoon cayenne pepper

3 pounds ripe tomatoes, cored, or 2 (28-ounce) cans whole tomatoes

$1/2$ cup finely chopped fresh cilantro

2 celery stalks, diced

3 tablespoons freshly squeezed lemon juice

3 tablespoons water

2 tablespoons white wine vinegar

Kosher salt to taste

Lemon slices; chopped parsley, chives, cilantro, or scallion greens; toasted pine nuts, for garnish

Heat the olive oil in a small saucepan over low heat. Add the garlic, paprika, cumin, and cayenne and cook until fragrant, 2 to 3 minutes. Set aside.

Chop the fresh tomatoes and put them through a food mill to remove the skins. If using canned tomatoes, cut off the hard stem ends; chop the tomatoes finely.

Transfer the tomatoes to a large bowl. Stir in the garlic mixture and the cilantro, celery, lemon juice, water, and vinegar. Season to taste with salt. Cover and refrigerate until ready to serve. Garnish individual servings with chopped herbs, scallions, and/or pine nuts.

TOASTED PARSLEYED PITA CRISPS

These buttery little triangles toasted with parsley and sesame seeds act as good scoops, but they don't necessarily need any accompaniment.

SERVES 6 TO 8

$1/4$ cup ($1/2$ stick) butter, softened

4 (6-inch) pita rounds, split and cut into triangles (8 to 10 per round)

2 tablespoons sesame seeds

2 tablespoons chopped fresh parsley

Preheat the oven to 300°F.

Spread the butter on the pita wedges and sprinkle generously with the sesame seeds and parsley. Place the pitas on an ungreased cookie sheet and bake until golden brown, 8 to 10 minutes. Serve warm.

STRAWBERRY FOOL

3 cups fresh strawberries,
washed and hulled
(frozen strawberries can
be substituted)

$^1/_2$ cup sugar

$1^1/_2$ tablespoons freshly
squeezed lemon juice

$1^1/_2$ teaspoons unflavored gelatin
powder (from 1 envelope)

1 cup heavy cream, well
chilled

"Fool" seems just right for the insanity of a Runamuck week. It's actually the name of a classic frothy English dessert made with mashed fresh berries folded into whipped cream. You can make raspberry, peach, nectarine, kiwi, or any kind of fruit fool the same way. Serve it with Icebox Sugar Cookies (page 82).

PHOTOGRAPH ON PAGE 83

SERVES 6 TO 8

Set aside a few perfect strawberries to use as garnish. In the bowl of a food processor, add the remaining strawberries, the sugar, and lemon juice and process until pureed. Transfer the mixture to a medium saucepan and sprinkle the gelatin on top. Let stand until the gelatin dissolves, about 15 minutes.

Place the saucepan over low heat and heat until warmed, 2 to 3 minutes. Refrigerate in a large bowl, covered, for at least 2 hours or overnight.

When nearly ready to serve, whip the cream in the medium bowl of an electric mixer until stiff peaks form. Fold the whipped cream into the chilled strawberry mixture. Refrigerate for at least 30 minutes.

To serve, spoon the fool into parfait glasses or wineglasses and garnish with the reserved strawberries.

ICEBOX SUGAR COOKIES

1 cup (2 sticks) unsalted
butter, softened

2 cups sugar

2 large eggs

1 teaspoon pure vanilla
extract

3 cups all-purpose flour

Pinch of kosher salt

Our grandmothers remember the days when a delivery man would drive through the neighborhood placing blocks of ice in the bottoms of families' iceboxes. These old-fashioned cookies got their name long ago when cooks would prepare cookie dough in advance, shape it into a log, and store it in the icebox. Then, it was easy to slice and bake small amounts. Keep some dough in your "icebox" and use it anytime you get the yen.

MAKES 4 TO 5 DOZEN 2-INCH COOKIES

In a medium bowl with an electric mixer, cream the butter and $1^1/_2$ cups sugar until light and fluffy, about 4 minutes. Add the eggs, one at a time, and beat well. Stir in the vanilla. Add the flour and salt and mix well.

Divide the dough into 3 parts. With your hands, roll each piece into a 3-inch-diameter log. Wrap the logs tightly with plastic wrap, then with aluminum foil; store in the refrigerator (icebox) or freezer until ready to bake.

Preheat the oven to 375°F.

Remove a log of cookie dough from the refrigerator or freezer and cut it into $^1/_4$- to $^1/_2$-inch slices. Place the remaining $^1/_2$ cup sugar on a plate. Dip one side of each cookie in the sugar and place the cookie, sugar side up, on a cookie sheet.

Bake the cookies until lightly browned, 20 to 25 minutes, depending on the thickness of the slices. Remove the cookies from the sheet while still warm and cool on a rack.

Strawberry Fool (page 81) with Icebox Sugar Cookies

RIVER WALK: *In summer, the low water level can accommodate even the most hesitant visitor.*

UNSCRIPTED MOMENTS

THE FIRST TIME I INVITED MY BROTHERS AND SISTERS AND their families to the ranch for a family reunion, I promised that it would be like a camp. It was. We called it Camp Runamuck the first time, and the name has stuck.

I'm sure that my grown-up idea of camp originated from my childhood, when my parents loaded the family into our Buick station wagon and headed north to the Minnesota lake country for our annual summer vacation. The resort was low-key, with bare-minimum cabins, but the swimming, horseback riding, fishing, and boating suited our interests perfectly. My parents, Merritt and Vivian Auld, didn't live to see our ranch or to participate in any of the reunions here. As the oldest child, I assumed the leadership role; that's when I summoned my two sisters, Leslie and Heather, and my two brothers, Guy and Kevin, to Montana. Maybe they, too, had echoes of our childhood holidays in mind when they accepted my invitation.

It's camp, all right. The days need some kind of structure, sleeping quarters need to be arranged, meals need to be coordinated. Activities are organized and semi-organized, and sometimes disorganized. We set a time for adults to be with the little kids for riding in the ring, but the teenagers all know how to groom and saddle, so they're more or less on their own. Most of our ranch horses are well known to the family, since the horses have been with us for a long time. One of our steadiest, most reliable guys, an old Arab named Ahab, is my nephew August's favorite—even after Ahab unceremoniously dumped him in the alley next to the barn one year, causing all the girls to kid him mercilessly. (Ahab, by the way, had never done that before, nor has he since, so we're still wondering about August's "technique.")

We organize hikes every day and pack lunches or, at least, our homemade "gorp" (trail mix) before heading for a trailhead in the Beartooth Absaroka National Forest just five miles up the road. And there's rafting, swimming, and fishing to round out the days.

Arts and crafts have always played a big role during our get-togethers as well. Although my sister Leslie teaches everything but art to sixth graders in Albuquerque, she loves bringing all the art supplies for flower pressing, tie-dyeing, rock painting, paper making, and so on for her nieces and nephew. It would seem as though there wouldn't be enough time for these projects, but they're left out in one room and worked on in between other, more "formal" activities.

For all the pride I take in assuming the role of camp director, I suspect that everyone's most vivid memories are inspired by the camp's unscripted moments. I recently received an e-mail from my niece Alex, who remembers "finding garden snakes; loping horses in the arena during a giant thunderstorm; having all-cousin sleepouts in the tent; completing jigsaw puzzles; making homemade paper with Aunt Leslie; learning about bears from a Yellowstone guide; doing yoga on the deck (including the frog, which none of the mothers could do!); and riding the four-wheeler all over the place!" She also remembers being diverted from a planned hike when I spotted huckleberries, and we spent hours picking them instead. Three pies' worth.

The number of attendees changes a bit each time, but there's always a great turnout. Some reunions have also included Tom's mother and his two brothers, my brother Kevin's in-laws, and friends we

HIGH OCTANE: *For the thrill-seeking six- to eight-year-old, there's plenty of current to push an inner tube.*

consider family as well. Thirty people may have been the largest number; twenty to twenty-five is the norm. It varies from year to year.

In addition to my sibs, the other regular is our father's sister, Aunt Marian, who is a retired pediatrician living in Arizona. She has always added spice to the family and, at age eighty-plus, still does. Marian's bluntness is well known. She speaks her mind and hides no feelings, a trait that would get anyone else in deep trouble. We all expect her eccentricities and would be disappointed without them. It was Marian, for example, who heard about the pig wrestling taking place at the Park County Fair one year and managed to get just about everybody at the reunion signed up as participants. (Pig wrestling is a timed event with four- or five-member teams all trying to catch a greased pig first.)

Not so organized are the impromptu hikes around the ranch property. Not so safe, either. Our daughter Jen's dog, Timber, was with a group going on a hike. They were at the top of a hill about a quarter mile from the farmhouse when my brother-in-law Bob heard a rattle. At first he thought it was the wind, but then he saw the coiled rattlesnake. He pointed and said, "Look," which made the dog go right for the snake. She was immediately bitten on the snout and hadn't taken more than a few steps when she started to stagger. Jen ran for help; Bob picked up this big, heavy Labrador and started walking home. Mind you, he wasn't used to

the altitude, never mind the hills. Meanwhile, another brother-in-law, Jim, jumped into cop-jock mode and into the driver's seat of the SUV. Jen took the dog from Bob and held him in the backseat while two more "helpers" piled in, and within seconds they were going seventy miles an hour along those winding gravel roads to Livingston.

It was the fastest seventeen-mile trip to town ever. The poor dog's muzzle had swelled to enormous proportions and she was having a hard time breathing, but in the end she made it because of Jim's fast driving and the vet's rapid intervention. Although I still believe the dog's life was in more danger on the trip to town.

If anything, for me the Runamucks mark, in a way that's both poignant and hopeful, the passage of time. The first generation of children have grown up, and now their children are lowering the average kid age again. The stick horses that neighed when their ears were squeezed have come out of the basement, as have the rubber balls with handles and the horse heads that are ideal for two-year-old bouncers. Sand toys for riverbank digging and the sheet of vinyl that's good for slipping and sliding when the garden hose runs on it emerge from the old barn loft where they've been stored. We've even added a permanent wooden play structure on the lawn in front of the lodge—swings, a slide, a climbing apparatus, and gymnastic rings—in anticipation of a growing family, and of many more Runamucks.

It's amazing to me to see so many members of my family gather for meals during these reunions. Given the numbers and the potential for chaos, we keep the food simple. We barbecue almost every night: hamburgers, buffalo dogs, chicken. There's always a green salad because (a) the garden is full of spinach and lettuce; (b) guests can help harvest, wash, and prepare it easily; and (c) it goes with good olive oil and vinegar and with all the menus. It's summer at its freshest.

These simple meals also allow us plenty of time just to sit on the porch, talking. I remove my metaphorical camp director's hat and we go anywhere—past, present, future.

To the delight of all the children, at the ranch there's usually an equal number of barn cats to play with (opposite). And Abbie is always up for her own form of catch and release (above): She always lets them go!

MEXICAN FIESTA

TOM'S SUNSET MARGARITAS

CHILES RELLENOS

RUNNING-W-BAR GUACAMOLE

HOMEMADE TORTILLA CHIPS

CHOPPED TOMATO SALSA

QUESADILLA BITES

TOM'S SUNSET MARGARITAS

3 to 4 tablespoons margarita
  salt

1 lime, cut into wedges

1 cup ice

1 (8-ounce) can frozen
  limeade concentrate

8 ounces good-quality tequila

4 ounces triple sec

When the sun starts to set and people are coming over to visit, Tom gets into his frozen-margaritas mode. He gets out the blender and starts to putter in the kitchen, knowing full well that his drinks will jump-start the evening. He says that everyone these days claims to be a margarita expert but that his recipe is the real deal. His enthusiasm is catching, and we all get to work on hors d'oeuvres to go along.

PHOTOGRAPH ALSO ON PAGE 92

SERVES 6 TO 8

To prepare the glasses: Place the margarita salt on a large sheet of waxed paper. Rub the rims of 6 or 8 margarita glasses with a lime wedge. Dip the rims in the mound of salt. Place the glasses in the freezer until ready to use.

    To make the margaritas: Put the ice in a blender; add the limeade concentrate, tequila, and triple sec. Blend until the ice is chopped up. Pour into the prepared chilled, salted glasses.

CHILES RELLENOS

FILLING

1¹/₂ cups low-fat ricotta cheese

²/₃ cup crumbled feta cheese

²/₃ cup firmly packed grated sharp white cheddar cheese

1 large garlic clove, pressed through a garlic press

2 tablespoons minced fresh cilantro

1 tablespoon minced fresh oregano

6 to 8 small poblano chiles

BATTER

6 cups canola oil

1 cup all-purpose flour

1 large egg yolk

¹/₂ teaspoon kosher salt

¹/₂ to 1 cup sparkling water, chilled

1 cup cornmeal

Many years ago Ellen took a course from Diana Kennedy, the well-known cook of Mexican cuisine. Diana taught the technique of making chiles rellenos, and although the filling varies from pueblo to pueblo, the general way to make them is the same. Poblano peppers are stuffed with a three-cheese filling and flavored with lots of fresh cilantro. The cornmeal-batter crust protects the filling and gives it some crunch. We often use our plentiful squash blossoms from zucchini plants instead of poblano peppers to stuff.

PHOTOGRAPH ON PAGES 92 AND 93

SERVES 6 TO 8

In a large mixing bowl using a fork, lightly mash the ricotta cheese, feta cheese, and cheddar cheese. Add the garlic, cilantro, and oregano and mix to make a light paste.

With a sharp knife, cut an opening down one side of each poblano and remove the seeds. The opening creates a pocket to hold the filling. Stuff each chile with 3 to 4 tablespoons filling.

Heat the oil in a large heavy skillet over medium-high heat until hot but not smoking. In a shallow dish, whisk the flour, egg yolk, and salt with enough sparkling water to make a batter the consistency of heavy cream. Place the cornmeal in another shallow dish.

Dip each stuffed chile into the batter and let the excess drip off. Dredge in the cornmeal and set aside.

When the oil is ready (a drop of water will "spit"), slide the chiles into the oil, one at a time. Cook, turning once, until nicely browned on all sides. Remove each chile carefully with a slotted spoon and drain on paper towels. Serve immediately.

BLOWING HOT AND COLD:
Chilled margaritas (page 90) are
the perfect complement to Chiles
Rellenos (page 91), best eaten hot and
oozing cheese. Our own guacamole
(page 94) and tortilla chips (page 94)
add to the festivities.

RUNNING-W-BAR GUACAMOLE

The western charm in this guacomole recipe is the straightforward simplicity of the lime juice and the fresh cilantro. The homemade tortilla chips are a must.

PHOTOGRAPH ON PAGES 92–93

MAKES 3 CUPS

3 ripe avocados, halved and pitted (reserve 1 pit)

1 cup chopped fresh cilantro or basil leaves

1/4 cup chopped scallions, green and white parts

1/4 cup chopped tomatoes (optional)

2 to 3 tablespoons freshly squeezed lime or lemon juice

1 to 2 teaspoons finely chopped fresh jalapeño pepper (optional)

2 garlic cloves, minced

Kosher salt and freshly ground black pepper to taste

Homemade Tortilla Chips (recipe follows), prepared tortilla chips, toast, or crackers, for serving

With a spoon, scoop the avocado flesh out of the peels into a medium-size bowl. With a fork, coarsely mash the avocados. Gently stir in the cilantro, scallions, tomatoes (if using), lime juice, jalapeño (if using), and garlic. Season to taste with salt and pepper.

Push the reserved pit into the middle of the mixture to keep the mixture from turning brown. Cover the bowl with plastic wrap; refrigerate until ready to serve with tortilla chips, toast, or crackers for scooping.

HOMEMADE TORTILLA CHIPS

Make your own chips out of fresh tortillas, and everyone will ask where you got them. They're just better by far than any brand and so simple to make. If you want wide strips instead of triangles, cut them in that shape. It's all the same as long as they are big enough to scoop up the dip.

PHOTOGRAPH ON PAGES 92–93

MAKES 30 CHIPS

5 to 6 (5-inch) yellow corn tortillas

Canola oil

Kosher salt

Preheat the oven to 325°F.

Cut each tortilla into 6 wedges. Brush with the oil and place on a cookie sheet. Bake until hardened and crisp, 20 to 30 minutes. Sprinkle with salt as you remove them from the oven. Serve warm with guacamole or your favorite dip.

CHOPPED TOMATO SALSA

This must be made fresh and served within several hours. Otherwise the salsa isn't crunchy.

MAKES 1¹/₂ CUPS

1 cup finely chopped tomatoes (about 2 medium)

2 tablespoons finely chopped onion

1 tablespoon seeded, chopped jalapeño pepper

1 tablespoon finely chopped fresh parsley

1 tablespoon finely chopped fresh cilantro

1 tablespoon olive oil

1 medium garlic clove, minced

In a pretty bowl, combine the tomatoes, onion, jalapeño, parsley, cilantro, oil, and garlic. Mix the salsa lightly with a fork. Cover with plastic wrap and refrigerate until ready to serve, up to 3 hours.

QUESADILLA BITES

While quesadillas are a good lunch dish, they're also good with cocktails before dinner. There are so many fillings to use in creating your very own version, but this basic recipe is always a winner.

SERVES 6 TO 8

2 to 4 tablespoons canola oil

16 (8-inch) flour tortillas

2 cups grated Jack cheese

FILLINGS

24 avocado slices (from about 2 avocados)

¹/₂ cup (¹/₄-inch-thick) green chile strips

¹/₄ cup chopped jalapeño peppers

¹/₂ cup thinly sliced grilled chicken

¹/₂ cup crumbled crisp bacon

¹/₂ cup crumbled browned sausage

1 cup sour cream, for serving

Chopped Tomato Salsa (above), for serving

Heat 1 teaspoon oil in a medium heavy skillet over medium heat until hot but not smoking. Place 1 tortilla in the skillet. Sprinkle with about 3 tablespoons grated cheese, then add a few tablespoons of whatever you would like from the list of fillings at left. Place another tortilla on top and cook the quesadilla, turning once and adding more oil if necessary, until browned on both sides. Transfer to paper towels to drain.

Repeat with the remaining tortillas, varying the fillings. Cut the quesadillas into wedges and serve immediately with sour cream and salsa.

TIME ON HOLD

THERE'S A MOMENT AT THE END OF THE DAY IN THE WEST WHEN the setting sun paints the valleys and foothills in soft shadows and washes the mountain peaks in a rosy patina. It's just a moment at the end of the day, but it's so amazing that it has its very own name: alpenglow. It's not a light show for tourists; it's a connection to those who have gone before, the American Indians and the early settlers who shared this moment as well. For me, it's when time seems suspended. Serenity prevails. Mother Earth is about to say good night and remind us once again of her majesty and our humble place in her presence. It's always a moment for personal reflection, to be at one with the wild creatures, to be absorbed by the beauty and the ancient origins of this landscape, to be deeply grateful to have a small place beneath this big sky.

The day makes a vivid retreat behind the mountains in the glorious haze of alpenglow.

COZY INDOOR DINNER

ONION PUFFS

CREAMY POLENTA
WITH WILD MUSHROOMS

SESAME-SOY VENISON CHOPS

WALNUT BRUSSELS SPROUTS

CRANBERRY AND PEAR RELISH

GINGERBREAD WITH WHIPPED CREAM

ONION PUFFS

Just the right size for a bite to go with a glass of wine before dinner. (Larger pieces work for lunch with a salad or soup.) They're almost too easy for words, but when life gets busy, we need recipes like this. For spicier puffs, spread some McLeod Hot Mustard (page 198) on the onion.

SERVES 6 TO 8

5 slices good-quality white bread

1/2 cup mayonnaise

1 small onion, thinly sliced

1/4 cup grated Parmesan cheese

Preheat the broiler.

Toast the bread lightly in a toaster. Cut off the crusts and cut the bread slices into quarters. Spread each quarter with mayonnaise and top with an onion slice. Spread a little more mayo on the onion and sprinkle with Parmesan.

Broil 3 to 4 inches from the heat until golden brown, just a few seconds; watch the puffs carefully to keep them from burning. Serve hot.

CREAMY POLENTA WITH WILD MUSHROOMS

In spring wild morel mushrooms appear throughout the woods around us. We're not always lucky enough to find them, but we have friends who always share their bounty because they know how much we appreciate morels. They're a perfect addition to lots of dishes, but polenta, perhaps, embraces them more than any other medium.

SERVES 6 TO 8

7 cups water

2 cups coarsely ground cornmeal

2 teaspoons virgin olive oil

2 cups sliced wild or cultivated morel mushrooms

2 (4-ounce) cans whole green chiles, drained and sliced into 1/2-inch strips

Freshly ground black pepper to taste

1 cup grated Jack cheese

3 tablespoons finely chopped fresh parsley or chives, for garnish

In a medium saucepan over high heat, bring the water and 1 teaspoon salt to a roiling boil. Slowly stir in the cornmeal. Reduce the heat and cook, stirring, until the polenta is thick and begins to pull away from the sides of the pan, 15 to 20 minutes. Set aside.

In a medium skillet over medium heat, heat the olive oil. Add the mushrooms and cook, stirring, until lightly browned, about 4 minutes. Add the chiles and cook until heated through. Add a few grinds of fresh pepper to taste.

Stir the cheese into the warm polenta until melted. Gently fold in the mushrooms and chiles. Spoon the polenta into a serving bowl and keep warm until ready to serve. Garnish with chopped parsley or chives.

BE PREPARED

Winter's crystal-white patina can make the extreme cold bearable and beautiful. The dry air takes away some of the sting.

FACT NO. 1: A sunny day can turn cloudy in a matter of minutes. If you're out on the plains, you can actually watch various weather systems coming and going all around; however, in the mountains or in a basin surrounded by mountains, the weather sneaks up on you. A squall or a thunderstorm can be minutes away from blinding hot sun.

FACT NO. 2: It can snow any month of the year in Montana; the temperature swings can be sixty degrees or more in a single day.

FACT NO. 3: Wind is always a part of the local weather forecast. It's welcome in winter, when the warm—well, relatively warm, for Montana—Chinook winds blow in and melt the snow-covered grasses, making foraging easier for livestock and wildlife. Summer winds, on the other hand, dry out the land and can be a menace during the fire season, late summer into fall.

FACT NO. 4: As the Scouts say, Be prepared. Planning for outdoor activities requires weather astuteness. You walk out the front door anticipating "nothing but blue skies all day long" and twenty minutes later the thunderheads that have been building out of sight behind the mountains have moved in and it begins to pour. Anyone taking hikes or rides into the mountains should pack rain gear in his or her backpack or saddlebags. Anyone preparing for an outdoor picnic dinner should always have a plan B, a place to retreat to in case the thunderclouds move in or the famous Montana winds start to blow. As for that thermos full of ice-cold lemonade—good idea. Now bring along a second one, full of steaming hot coffee. Just in case.

SESAME-SOY VENISON CHOPS

Wild game meat has very little fat, so it benefits from a good marinade that will tenderize and add moisture.

Ellen has shot deer in Georgia, where it's quite legal; butchered the animal herself; and cooked it for a formal dinner party. It turns out she's a great shot. One time in the pouring rain she went out with a ranch hand on Little St. Simon Island; no one thought she'd get anything. But they were wrong: She shot four deer with four shots. Never underestimate the ability of a city girl if she has good aim and no buck fever—the inability to pull the trigger.

SERVES 6 TO 8

MARINADE

1 cup red wine

2 tablespoons soy sauce

2 tablespoons sesame oil

1 tablespoon balsamic vinegar

1 garlic clove, crushed

2 tablespoons finely chopped fresh rosemary leaves

1 teaspoon sugar

12 to 14 (4- to 5-ounce) venison chops, single rib, or backstrap venison without the bone (more of a medallion)

For the marinade: In a small saucepan over medium-low heat, heat the wine, soy sauce, sesame oil, vinegar, garlic, rosemary, and sugar for 3 minutes. Remove the saucepan from the heat and let cool.

Place the chops in a large bowl and add the marinade, turning to coat. Cover and refrigerate, turning the chops occasionally, for an hour or 2.

Meanwhile, prepare a hot grill or preheat the broiler. Place the chops on the grill rack 4 to 6 inches over direct heat. For medium, cook for 6 to 8 minutes, turning once. Or broil 2 inches from the heat, turning once, for 6 to 8 minutes.

WALNUT BRUSSELS SPROUTS

I tried this recipe one Thanksgiving years ago, and because it was such a hit, I've been making it ever since. The walnuts and walnut oil give the sprouts such a new dimension that they turn into quite a different-tasting vegetable. Don't wait for a holiday to try it.

SERVES 6 TO 8

3 (10-ounce) containers fresh Brussels sprouts, cleaned

$^1/_2$ cup chopped walnuts

$^1/_3$ cup walnut oil

Few drops of balsamic vinegar

Kosher salt and freshly ground black pepper to taste

Wash and trim the ends of each Brussels sprout. Separate the leaves of the sprouts and place them in a bowl. This can be time consuming—if you like, separate the large outer leaves and shred the core with a sharp knife.

Heat a large cast-iron skillet over high heat. Add the walnuts and toast in the dry skillet, shaking the pan so they don't burn, 1 to 2 minutes. Transfer to a small bowl and set aside.

In the same skillet, heat the walnut oil over medium heat. Add the sprouts and cook, stirring gently, 3 to 4 minutes.

Transfer the sprouts to a serving dish. Sprinkle with walnuts and balsamic vinegar and season to taste with salt and pepper.

CRANBERRY AND PEAR RELISH

1 (16-ounce) bag fresh cranberries, or 1 (15-ounce) can whole cranberries

1 cup water

1$\frac{1}{2}$ cups sugar ($\frac{1}{2}$ cup if using canned cranberries)

3 to 4 unripe pears (Bartlett, Anjou, or Comice), peeled and diced

$\frac{1}{4}$ cup freshly squeezed lemon juice

$\frac{1}{4}$ teaspoon ground cinnamon

$\frac{1}{4}$ teaspoon ground allspice

With its cinnamon and allspice flavorings, this cranberry relish is a fine complement to the gentle pear and an excellent condiment to serve with chops, chicken, or roasts—even with scrambled eggs. And the color is a gorgeous deep burgundy that dresses up any table.

MAKES 5 TO 6 CUPS

Rinse and pick over the fresh cranberries, discarding stems and imperfect berries.

In a large saucepan, bring the water and sugar to a boil. Add the pears and simmer for 5 minutes. Add the cranberries and bring the mixture to a boil. Cook, stirring, until the berries start to pop, about 5 minutes.

Remove the pan from the heat and add the lemon juice, cinnamon, and allspice. Transfer to a bowl and let cool; cover and refrigerate overnight to thicken.

GINGERBREAD WITH WHIPPED CREAM

1 cup molasses

$\frac{1}{2}$ cup (1 stick) unsalted butter, softened

2$\frac{1}{3}$ cups all-purpose flour

$\frac{3}{4}$ teaspoon baking soda

1 teaspoon ground ginger

1 teaspoon ground cinnamon

$\frac{1}{4}$ teaspoon ground cloves

Pinch of kosher salt

1 cup sour cream

1 pint heavy cream, whipped with 1 teaspoon sugar, for serving

There's nothing like a helping of warm gingerbread to make people feel at home. The aroma of the gingerbread wafting from the oven as the cake bakes always takes me back to my childhood and memories of after-school snacks. Gingerbread's texture doesn't resemble any other cake or bread; it's moist, fine, and soft, and it should stick to the roof of your mouth. Whipped cream or cold applesauce on the side is part of the tradition—my tradition, at any rate.

MAKES 12 SQUARES

Preheat the oven to 350°F. Butter an 8-inch square glass baking pan.

In a small saucepan over medium-low heat, bring the molasses and butter to a boil. Remove from the heat, let cool, and set aside.

In a large bowl, sift together the flour, baking soda, ginger, cinnamon, cloves, and salt. Using an electric mixer on medium speed, beat in the molasses mixture and the sour cream; beat until the batter is smooth, about 2 minutes.

Pour the batter into the prepared pan; bake for 40 to 45 minutes, until a toothpick or cake tester inserted in the center comes out clean. Serve with the sweetened whipped cream.

SEASONS BY THE MINUTE

BY VERLYN KLINKENBORG

EVERY DAY THE SUNLIGHT INCREASES OR decreases by a certain amount. Every night the moon slides predictably a little farther behind in its route across the sky and shows a little more or less of itself. The stars pivot in perfect synchrony overhead. Earth moves around the sun like clockwork. But if the seasons moved as mechanically as that—like part of an elaborate medieval timepiece—they would be cruel, too precise for humans. We like a little nuance in time.

Every year brings the same weather to Montana—snow, rain, sun, heat, cold, and wind. And yet each year the weather scatters itself across the calendar just randomly enough to create the illusion that each year is a different year. What if the terrestrial pattern was as consistent as the astronomical pattern? We would know, every year, what day the Chinook blows, when the first frost comes, and the last frost. We would know the temperature of the coldest night and the hottest day and the exact dates of both. The leaves would come out in perfect order, year after year, and fall in perfect succession. The birds would return for an unbreakable appointment. The wolves would pup right on time. The garden would grow in perfect regimentation. And only the differences in ourselves, and in others, would allow us to tell the years apart.

But in Montana the calendar manages to be rigid and volatile at the same time. The borders of the growing season are absolute, and yet no one is ever really sure when the black frost is going to come. It can snow nearly any day of the year, and when the hard snow falls in autumn, you're fenced off from summer for a good long time. People who choose to live in Montana are people who revel in the possibilities of weather. They may complain about the tomatoes, but if they really wanted tomatoes, they'd live farther south. There's a certain dark pleasure in seeing your mild domestic hopes—a melon, just once—blighted by a spectacular cold front that makes the elk hunker down and the coyote bury its nose in its tail. To live in the weather shadow of the Absarokas is to clamor for the unexpected.

The result is that the Montana calendar has dozens of seasons. Some may last only a few minutes, but what they gain by their brevity is particularity, definition. No prolonged ripeness here. No tomorrow. None of the patient succulence of lower latitudes. The chokecherries come ripe. There is a flourish of birds and bears and humans. The season is over. The river boils with Baetis—drizzling, fifty degrees. Then the wind blows the sun into the sky, and the water goes flat and stays flat. New-hatched swallows fledge in haste to depart in haste.

A calendar like that—moment by moment—brings a kind of acerbity with it. You can taste it in almost everything that grows here—sour till it's sweet, and even then a memory of sour. Only the bees manage perfect sweetness. They compress their season into the shortest possible compass, and they're relentless in their search for the next bloom. A worker bee's day is one snap judgment after another. Ripe? Not ripe? The bees harvest the singular perfection of every blossom from one crop, one species of wildflower after another. They know how short the season is. That knowledge makes the honey what it is.

And yet the humans lay plans as though it were a clockwork year. Calves drop and lambs fall on cue, no matter what the weather has in store. Branding comes just when it always does, and so does gathering. By acceding to the regularity of the printed calendar—all those blank pages in the year ahead of us—we get to feel the volatility of the year all that more keenly. If ranchers knew they'd always be calving in an ice storm, they'd change the date of calving. But they don't know. If northern gardeners were sure they could never ripen a tomato, they'd give up tomatoes. But they aren't sure.

That's the game.

We hold to our patterns, knowing the weather won't. If we could take the weather just as it comes—suiting ourselves entirely to the conditions—we wouldn't really be human at all. We'd be midges, rising and sinking along the river's edge.

It's something to think about when you look up at the benches beneath the mountains and see those lights burning in the ranch houses. You can't slip very far behind the weather here and still stay in business. The firewood is long since stacked—hauled down from the forest permits months ago. The garden is long since put to bed under a layer of horse manure, compost, and straw. The machines that need oiling are oiled, and the pipes that need draining are drained. The shop is clean and ready for a long winter of welding once the snow starts to fly. The horses are fit to the season.

SHORT RIB FEAST

BEET AND ENDIVE SALAD

OVEN-ROASTED CARROTS, PARSNIPS,
AND POTATOES

DUTCH OVEN SHORT RIBS

BURNT-SUGAR PUMPKIN PIE

BEET AND ENDIVE SALAD

Growing certain crops is hard to do in Montana, but we've had a lot of success with root vegetables such as beets, which will grow all summer. This simple salad shows off all our varieties: the vibrant golden yellow and red ones, and the candy beets, with concentric circles like tree rings. Wrap the beet greens in paper towels and refrigerate. Then sauté them in olive oil and garlic for a terrific side dish.

SERVES 6 TO 8

6 to 8 medium-size beets (yellow, red, or mixed), trimmed

¹/₂ cup Balsamic Vinaigrette (page 152)

4 to 6 heads Belgian endive, trimmed and separated into leaves

3 tablespoons chopped fresh chives

Place the beets in a medium saucepan with enough water to cover by 2 inches. Bring to a boil over medium heat and cook, covered, until tender when pierced with a knife, 20 to 30 minutes. Drain.

Stick a fork in the cut end of a beet and place the beet under cool running water; with a sharp paring knife, scrape the skin away. Repeat with the remaining beets. Slice or quarter the beets (the pieces should be small enough to fit into the endive spears later). Place in a bowl, cover, and keep warm until serving.

Add the vinaigrette to the beets and toss to coat. Spoon the beets into the endive leaves, arrange on a serving platter, and garnish with the chives.

OVEN-ROASTED CARROTS, PARSNIPS, AND POTATOES

Oven-roasted vegetables drizzled with a little olive oil and sprinkled with a little coarse salt add up to a really good accompaniment. Tender, soft, and delicious.

SERVES 6 TO 8

6 carrots, trimmed and peeled

6 parsnips, trimmed and peeled

8 large new potatoes, peeled

3 tablespoons olive oil

1 tablespoon chopped fresh sage, marjoram, or oregano

Kosher salt and freshly ground black pepper to taste

Preheat the oven to 350°F.

Place the carrots, parsnips, and potatoes on a cookie sheet or in a shallow baking dish. Drizzle with olive oil and turn the vegetables to coat all sides. Sprinkle with the sage and salt and pepper to taste. Roast until tender when pierced with a fork, 40 to 50 minutes. (Toss with a spatula at least once while the vegetables are roasting.)

DUTCH OVEN SHORT RIBS

3 large eggs

1 cup seasoned flour
(see Note)

4 pounds beef short ribs,
trimmed and cut into
4- to 5-inch pieces

About 3 tablespoons butter

About 3 tablespoons
canola oil

5 garlic cloves, finely chopped

3/4 cup beef broth

1 cup canned tomato puree

5 tablespoons chopped fresh
parsley

1/4 cup chopped fresh cilantro

2 tablespoons chili powder

1 teaspoon ground cumin

1 or 2 whole dried red chile
peppers, depending on their
heat

16 (6- or 8-inch) corn tortillas
(optional)

In days gone by, if you could have choosen only one pot to use, the Dutch oven would have been the winner hands down. No other cooking implement has ever challenged its brilliance. The pot has been used to cook everything from stews to corn bread and cobblers since the early 1700s. Blacksmith Paul Revere designed some of these cast-iron pots, which were made throughout New England. Traders from Holland brought large quantities for barter with the Indians and the frontier settlers, hence the name. The pot can sit on top of a fire or hot coals or even be buried in the coals to simulate an oven. The lid can be inverted and used as a skillet to fry bacon, eggs, or pancakes. If you place a cup of water in the bottom of the pot, you can roast any meat or game to perfection. You'll agree after tasting these choice short ribs.

PHOTOGRAPH ON PAGE 206

SERVES 6 TO 8

Preheat the oven to 300°F.

Beat the eggs in a shallow bowl; place the seasoned flour on a plate. Dip the rib pieces in the beaten egg, then in the seasoned flour, shaking off any excess. In a large heavy skillet over medium-high heat, melt 2 tablespoons butter with 2 tablespoons oil until hot but not smoking. In batches, brown the ribs on both sides, adding more butter and oil if needed. Transfer the ribs to a Dutch oven or large casserole.

Add the garlic to the skillet and brown lightly. Add the broth, tomato puree, parsley, cilantro, chili powder, cumin, and chiles, scraping the browned bits from the bottom of the skillet. Add the broth mixture to the ribs. Cover the Dutch oven and bake, basting frequently, until the meat is very tender and falling off the bone, about 3 hours. Remove and discard the chiles.

If you like, serve the ribs with warmed tortillas: Butter the tortillas lightly on one side and stack them on top of one another. Wrap in aluminum foil and warm in a low oven until ready to serve.

NOTE: To make seasoned flour, combine 1 cup quick-mixing flour (such as Wondra) with 1 teaspoon *each* garlic salt, dried oregano, dried thyme, dried basil, and freshly ground black pepper.

BURNT-SUGAR PUMPKIN PIE

DOUGH

1³/₄ cups all-purpose flour

¹/₂ cup (1 stick) unsalted butter

¹/₄ cup cold vegetable shortening

Pinch of kosher salt

3 tablespoons ice water

FILLING

¹/₃ cup granulated sugar

1 cup light corn syrup

¹/₂ cup firmly packed dark brown sugar

2 tablespoons unsalted butter

3 large eggs

2 teaspoons pure vanilla extract

Pinch of kosher salt

1 cup canned pumpkin puree

¹/₂ teaspoon ground ginger

¹/₄ teaspoon ground nutmeg

¹/₄ teaspoon ground cinnamon

1 cup pecans, chopped

1 cup heavy cream, whipped, for serving

There are many times when I need to make a dessert but don't want to travel into town for groceries. Seventeen miles isn't that far, you say, but here it's a forty-minute trip on a dreaded washboard road that could knock your teeth out as you jiggle along. So I always keep canned pumpkin, frozen pecans, molasses, and sugar in the pantry. With its nutty caramelized crunch, this holiday dessert holds its own at any dinner.

SERVES 8 TO 10

To make the dough: In the bowl of a food processor, place the flour, butter, shortening, and salt; pulse on and off until the dough resembles coarse meal. Add the ice water and pulse again until the dough forms a ball. On a lightly floured surface, gently pat the dough into a flattened ball. Place the dough in a plastic bag and refrigerate for 1 hour.

On a lightly floured surface, roll out the dough to an 11-inch round, ¹/₄ inch thick. Transfer to a 9-inch pie plate; trim and crimp the edges. Refrigerate for at least 30 minutes.

To make the filling: In a heavy saucepan over medium-low heat, cook the granulated sugar until it is medium-dark brown, moving the pan constantly to prevent burning. Reduce the heat and stir in the corn syrup, brown sugar, and butter. Cook for another minute or two to combine. Remove from the heat and set aside to cool.

Preheat the oven to 350°F.

In a large bowl, whisk together the eggs, vanilla, and salt. Add the cooled syrup mixture in a slow steady stream, stirring to combine.

In another large bowl, combine the pumpkin, ginger, nutmeg, and cinnamon. Add all but ¹/₂ cup of the egg-sugar mixture.

Pour the filling into the chilled shell and arrange the chopped nuts on top. Spoon the remaining ¹/₂ cup egg-sugar mixture over the nuts.

Bake the pie on the center rack until the filling is set and the crust is pale golden, 45 to 50 minutes. Let the pie cool; serve with whipped cream.

IN THE MIDDLE OF NOWHERE

No, he's not going to ask for directions. In the vastness of Yellowstone, you'd better have a good idea of where you're going. Or a GPS.

THE NAME THOROFARE SOUNDS LIKE A BUSY avenue in a densely populated city, but in the West it's the name of the most remote area in the lower forty-eight states, a section of Yellowstone National Park that is home to large numbers of grizzlies, elk, and wolves. For ages, it's also been a popular game trail, and as early as 1830 fur traders were referring to this route as the Thorofare. In 1807 a famous frontiersman named John Coulter set his beaver traps all along this trail, and Rocky Mountain explorer Bob Marshall signed into the park station log in the early 1930s.

Horse thieves also made ingenious use of the remoteness of the place. From the 1860s to the 1880s, at least a couple of gangs stole horses in the south, altered brands in Jackson Hole, and drove the herd into the Thorofare and out into Cody, Wyoming, where they were sold. There the thieves would reverse the process: a new bunch of horses would be "acquired" and brands changed, and the herd would be driven into the Thorofare and out to Jackson Hole to the sale barn. U.S. Army scouts had their hands full trying to curtail this rustling stronghold. More than a century later, National Park rangers would patrol this region on horseback on the lookout for poachers, if not horse thieves.

Several summers ago, Tom and I had the chance to replicate a park ranger's day when we rode into this part of Yellowstone with two of its finest rangers, John Lounsberry and Doug Smith, along with three other supporters of the Yellowstone Park Foundation, a private organization developed by concerned citizens who are commited to preserving the infrastructure of the park. John, who was about to retire, had headed

that park district for many years. Doug had been in charge of the wolf reintroduction and was able to point out signs of wolf habitation that we would have completely missed. The area had been severely burned in 1988, and we were immediately struck by the ghostly nature of what used to be thick stands of dark green evergreens; in their place are pillars of tree trunks, looking like apocryphal sculptures. You see the topography and the boulders and the green moss and the wildflowers that grow on the forest floor, which you would never have seen before the mass of thick pines burned. Land that first seems barren gets more intricate and starkly beautiful the longer you're in it.

Getting around all the downfall was made easy for us because our group rode in on park horses. Believe me, it's worth the walk. If you're unwilling to hike or ride horseback, you're out of luck, as there are no roads.)

As prey animals, our horses need to be alert to any approaching danger. They constantly monitor the landscape; they're also curious and notice even slight changes in their environment, such as a fallen tree, another horse, or a person they haven't seen before.

CHOKECHERRY HARVEST

SAVORY PHYLLO SQUARES
WITH GOAT CHEESE AND SAGE

PORK TENDERLOIN
WITH CHOKECHERRY GLAZE

CHOKECHERRY JELLY

BAKED ACORN SQUASH

MARJORAM ONIONS

PEAR TATIN

SAVORY PHYLLO SQUARES
WITH GOAT CHEESE AND SAGE

Savory herbs such as thyme and oregano are good in this dish, but sage with goat cheese is my favorite, because it's so gentle. Most grocers carry phyllo dough in the freezer section, kind of an invitation to learn how to work with it. The thin leaves stick together when brushed with melted butter, but the pastry is very forgiving; it just requires a little practice. For this recipe, you will fill the whole cookie sheet using half the package of phyllo.

SERVES 6 TO 8

1/2 **cup (1 stick) unsalted butter, melted**

1 **(16-ounce) package 14- by 18-inch sheets frozen phyllo dough, thawed overnight in the refrigerator**

3/4 **cup crumbled goat cheese**

1/4 **teaspoon dried thyme**

1 **cup grated mozzarella cheese**

1 **cup thinly sliced onions**

12 **fresh sage leaves**

Kosher salt and freshly ground black pepper to taste

Preheat the oven to 375°F. Lightly brush a 15- by 13-inch cookie sheet with some of the melted butter.

Unroll the phyllo dough. Divide the stack of dough in half. Roll up one half, wrap it in plastic wrap, and return it to the refrigerator; reserve for another use. The thin sheets of phyllo dry out quickly, so to work with the dough, cover it with plastic wrap, then with a damp kitchen towel.

Place one sheet of phyllo on the prepared cookie sheet; brush with melted butter. Repeat twice, covering the entire cookie sheet and overlapping the phyllo in places. Sprinkle with 2 to 3 tablespoons goat cheese and a pinch of thyme. Repeat about four times, using all the goat cheese and all the phyllo in the stack.

Crimp the edges to form a rim. Sprinkle the mozzarella and onion slices on the dough. Arrange the sage leaves about 3 inches apart so that when the phyllo is cut into squares, there will be one sage leaf per square. Season with salt and pepper. Drizzle any leftover butter on top.

Bake the phyllo until golden brown, 45 to 50 minutes. Transfer to a cutting board and cut into twelve 2-inch squares.

PORK TENDERLOIN WITH CHOKECHERRY GLAZE

Any jelly or sweet sauce will create a crunchy glaze on a roast or on poultry. While chokecherry jelly is usually served with biscuits or bread, it's also a perfect glaze for pork tenderloin, sealing in the juices and crisping the skin.

PHOTOGRAPH ON PAGE 124

SERVES 4 TO 6

4 tablespoons good-quality olive oil

2 tablespoons chopped fresh parsley

4 medium garlic cloves, minced

Kosher salt and freshly ground black pepper to taste

2 (2-pound) pork tenderloins, butterflied

1 cup seasoned flour (see Note)

2 medium onions, peeled and quartered

1 cup Chokecherry Jelly (page 125), or jelly or jam of your choice

3 tablespoons white or red wine

2 cups beef broth

2 tablespoons quick-mixing flour (such as Wondra)

Preheat the oven to 450°F.

In a small bowl, make a paste out of 2 tablespoons olive oil and the parsley, garlic, salt, and pepper.

Unroll the pork loins and spread the insides with the garlic paste. Roll up the loins and tie with kitchen twine. Dredge in the seasoned flour.

Heat the remaining 2 tablespoons olive oil in a large skillet over high heat. Add the loins and sear on all sides. Transfer to a roasting pan and add the quartered onions.

Brush the loins with the jelly. Roast, basting with the pan juices a few times, until an instant-read thermometer inserted in the thickest parts registers 155°F, 30 to 40 minutes. Remove the loins and place on a warm plate.

To make the gravy, add the wine and broth to the pan, scraping any browned bits from the bottom. Sprinkle with the flour, scraping and whisking until the gravy is the consistency of tomato juice. Strain the gravy through a fine-mesh sieve.

To serve, slice the loins into 1/2-inch-thick diagonal pieces, discarding the twine. Transfer to dinner plates and add a few pieces of onion and a ladle of gravy to each serving.

NOTE: To make seasoned flour, combine 1 cup quick-mixing flour (such as Wondra) with 1 teaspoon *each* garlic salt, dried oregano, dried thyme, dried basil, and freshly ground black pepper.

CHOKECHERRY JELLY

14 to 16 cups fresh chokecherries (enough to fill a gallon pail), or store-bought (see Selected Sources)

1 (1¾-ounce) package fruit pectin

3 to 4 cups sugar

We make chokecherry jelly every year. The berries are sour when they're freshly picked at the end of summer, but after they're made into jelly, the taste is sweet and delicious, the color a brilliant amethyst, like no other. If you don't have chokecherries growing near you, you can order them or substitute any sour cherry in this recipe.

PHOTOGRAPH ALSO ON PAGE 127

MAKES 10 TO 14½ ONE-PINT JARS

Wash the chokecherries and discard any stems. Put in a very large pot and gently mash to break open the berries slightly. Add cold water to cover and bring to a boil over medium-high heat. Reduce the heat to low, cover, and simmer for 10 to 15 minutes.

To remove the pits and skin, strain the liquid through a colander lined with cheesecloth. You should have 10 to 12 cups juice.

Combine 3½ cups juice with the fruit pectin in a large pot. Bring to a boil over high heat, stirring occasionally. Add the sugar and return the jelly to a full boil; boil for 1 minute, stirring constantly.

Remove from the heat and skim off any foam with a spoon. Pour at once into sterilized jars (see Note), leaving ½ inch of headroom. Cover with sterilized new lids and screw rims. Cool in a draft-free place.

Place the jars on a rack in the canning pot to keep them from sitting directly on the bottom of the pan. Cover with water, at least 2 inches above the jars. Bring to a boil; boil for 10 minutes at a rolling boil (timing from the start of the boil).

Carefully transfer the jars to a work surface covered with a kitchen towel. Let cool for 12 to 24 hours. Test the jars for a good seal.

NOTE: To sterilize the jars and lids, wash them in your dishwasher before filling them with the jelly. To make absolutely sure your jars are sterile, pour boiling water over them, including the canning lids, called the flats, and rims.

COLOR THEM DELICIOUS:
Chokecherry branches are red
with promise (above). Made into
a sweet jelly, they taste as good
as they look (opposite).

THE BITTERSWEET BERRY

THEY MAY NOT BE THE QUEEN OF ALL BERRIES—PERSONALLY, I'd reserve that crown for the wondrous huckleberry—but the wild chokecherries *(Prunus virginiana)* that grow in our neck of the woods are at least royalty.

The bushes on which they grow are scrubby and low, thriving mainly along dirt roads, riverbeds, and creeks, not the kind of shrub you'd find in a manicured garden. When the fruit ripens in late August, the deep purple berries look luscious, but only the bears find them appetizing. They're puckery-tart, and they have a small pit in the center—surely where the name *choke* originates—that makes the initial taste eye-watering and not very palatable. Cooking them makes the difference.

Laden with vitamin C, chokecherries played an integral role in the diet of the Plains Indians. The Crow, who used the area as summer hunting grounds, carried with them pemmican, a highly nutritious dried food made with chokecherries and venison or bison meat. American Indians and pioneers refrained from eating other parts of the bush, which were toxic, but they did use a bark infusion as a medicinal external wash.

Today, it's still a race with the bears to harvest the berries because, when sweetened, the berries make the most delectable jelly. It's a pleasing end-of-summer project; but it's bittersweet for me, too, just as the fruit is, because it almost always coincides with the time to leave the ranch and head back to the city.

Chokecherry Jelly (page 125)

PEAR TATIN

A tarte tatin is an upside-down fruit pie. The fruit, sugar, and butter are cooked in a cast-iron skillet on top of the stove until the fruit caramelizes. Then a crust is placed on top and it's all baked in the oven until browned. The pie is inverted on a plate, and the dessert is complete. Tartes tatin are typically made with apples, but pears are a nice variation.

SERVES 6 TO 8

DOUGH

1³/₄ cups all-purpose flour

Pinch of baking powder

Pinch of kosher salt

¹/₂ cup (1 stick) unsalted butter, cut up

2 tablespoons sugar

1 large egg yolk

2 to 3 tablespoons ice water

FILLING

2 pounds (4 to 5) firm pears (Anjou or Bosc)

Juice of 1 lemon

1 cup sugar

¹/₄ cup (¹/₂ stick) unsalted butter

Heavy cream, whipped, for serving

To make the dough: In the bowl of a food processor, combine the flour, baking powder, and salt. Add the cut-up butter and the sugar and pulse until the mixture resembles coarse meal. Mix the egg yolk and ice water together in a small bowl; add to the flour mixture. Pulse until the dough comes together in a ball. On a lightly floured surface, gently pat the dough into disk. Wrap the dough in plastic and refrigerate for at least 30 minutes.

To make the filling: Peel, halve lengthwise, and core the pears. Cut lengthwise slices, about three to each pear half. Place the slices in a bowl; add the lemon juice and toss. Add ¹/₄ cup sugar and toss again. Set aside.

Melt the butter in a 10-inch heavy ovenproof skillet over medium heat. Add the remaining ³/₄ cup sugar and cook until the mixture caramelizes, 6 to 8 minutes. Stir and remove from the heat before it gets too brown; it will continue to brown while off the heat.

Drain the pears; carefully arrange the slices in the skillet with the fat ends at the outside of the pan, the narrow ends in the center. Cook the pears over medium-low heat until there is no liquid in the pan, only very thick sauce, 15 minutes or longer. The trick to this recipe is to reduce the juices in the skillet so that the pears are thick enough to invert onto the crust, without being watery.

Preheat the oven to 375°F.

On a lightly floured surface, roll out the dough to a 10-inch round, ¹/₄ inch thick; place on top of the pears, pressing down very gently. Bake in the lower third of the oven until the pastry is golden brown, about 25 minutes. Remove the tatin from the oven and let sit for about 20 minutes to settle.

Place a serving plate over the skillet and invert the tatin onto it, with the pastry on the bottom. Spoon the thickened juices from the skillet over the top. Cut into wedges and serve warm with whipped cream.

OSSO BUCO BANQUET

VICHYSSOISE WITH CHIVES

BISON OSSO BUCO

SWEETGRASS COUNTRY BREAD

GARDEN PEAS AND ORZO
WITH FRESH MINT

MEYER LEMON MERINGUE PIE

VICHYSSOISE WITH CHIVES

3 large Idaho or Russet
potatoes

5 tablespoons unsalted butter

3 to 4 medium leeks,
white parts only

6 cups strong chicken stock

2 cups (1 pint) heavy cream

Kosher salt and freshly
ground white pepper
to taste

$^1/_2$ cup chopped fresh chives,
for garnish

There is nothing better to start off a summer meal, or any meal for that matter, than a bowl of chilled or warmed potato-leek soup. At the ranch, we pass bunches of our homegrown chives around the table—and cut away to our hearts' content. Of course, for a more formal presentation, the garnishing can be done in the kitchen before serving.

SERVES 8 TO 10

Peel the potatoes and cut them into 1-inch cubes. Place in a large pot of salted water and cook until tender, about 12 minutes. Drain and set aside.

Meanwhile, split the leeks lengthwise and wash them well in cold water, making sure that the sand is out. Cut them into pieces and set them aside to dry.

Melt the butter in a skillet over medium heat. When the pan is hot, add the leeks and sauté, stirring, until they are opaque, about 4 minutes.

Add the chicken stock and bring to a boil. Lower the heat and simmer until tender, about 10 minutes. Add the potatoes, season with salt and pepper, and toss to coat.

Put the mixture, in batches, in a food processor or blender and process until smooth. Stir in the cream.

Transfer the soup to a large bowl and chill in the refrigerator for 3 to 4 hours or overnight.

When ready to serve, taste again for seasonings. Garnish each bowl with 2 teaspoons of chopped chives or pass the chives for people to garnish their own. Serve the soup cold or hot.

BISON OSSO BUCO

This recipe originated at one of the Turner bison ranches. Ted Turner, who is largely responsible for reintroducing buffalo to the prairie, has also played a culinary role by opening specialty restaurants all over the country, restaurants that serve primarily bison, prepared all different ways. A bison shank is a rather large bone that has to be cut up so that it fits into a pan. The meat is lean, has very little fat, and is extremely tender. And the marrow—luscious huge pieces of it—is a delicacy in our household. This is a slow-cooking dish, so you have time to take a hike and do other things while it's in the oven.

Bison shank can be obtained where bison are indigenous and through some mail-order sources. If you can't get bison shank, you can use veal shanks or lamb shanks.

SERVES 6 TO 8

6 or 8 (1-pound) bison shanks (see Selected Sources), or veal or lamb shanks

1 cup seasoned flour (see Note)

3 tablespoons olive oil

4 cups chicken stock, plus more if needed

²/₃ cup white wine

¹/₄ cup chopped fresh parsley

2 tablespoons chopped fresh sage

1 sprig fresh rosemary

8 medium garlic cloves, crushed and peeled

Preheat the oven to 350°F.

Dredge the shanks in the seasoned flour. Heat the olive oil in a large heavy skillet over medium-high heat. Add the shanks and brown on all sides. Transfer them to a large casserole dish.

Add the stock, wine, parsley, sage, rosemary, and garlic to the casserole. Bake for 2 hours. Reduce the heat to 300°F and bake, basting the shanks occasionally to keep them tender and moist, and adding more stock if necessary, until the meat is tender and falling from the bone, 4 to 6 hours longer.

NOTE: To make seasoned flour, combine 1 cup quick-mixing flour (such as Wondra) with 1 teaspoon *each* garlic salt, dried oregano, dried thyme, dried basil, and freshly ground black pepper.

Bison Osso Buco alongside Garden Peas and Orzo with Fresh Mint (page 140)

SWEETGRASS COUNTRY BREAD

Breads such as this one are filled with grains and other healthful ingredients. We make homemade bread to serve with any meal. Freshly baked bread from a home kitchen is a rare thing in these days of fast food and quick fixes. And there is a tinge of self-righteousness about its contributions to everyone's health.

MAKES 1 LOAF

1 envelope (2$^1/_4$ teaspoons) active dry yeast

3 tablespoons tepid water

2$^1/_2$ cups bread flour

3 tablespoons coarse cornmeal

3 tablespoons rolled oats

3 tablespoons wheat bran

3 tablespoons brown sugar

1$^1/_2$ teaspoons kosher salt

About 1 cup water

$^1/_3$ cup buttermilk

6 tablespoons sunflower seeds, plus 2 tablespoons for topping

1$^1/_2$ tablespoons honey

Butter a 12- by 5- by 3-inch bread loaf pan.

To proof the yeast: In a small bowl, combine the yeast with the tepid water. (Tepid water is just under 100°F. Test it by putting your pinky finger in the water; if you cannot feel anything, the temperature is right.) The mixture will bubble when it is active.

In the large bowl of an electric mixer, combine the flour, cornmeal, oats, bran, brown sugar, and salt. Add the yeast mixture. In a medium bowl, combine $^1/_2$ cup water, the buttermilk, honey, and the 6 tablespoons sunflower seeds. Add the wet ingredients. Using the dough hook, mix on medium (add more water if needed) until elastic and shiny, 5 to 10 minutes.

Turn out the dough on a lightly floured surface and knead until the dough is well worked, about 10 minutes. The dough should not tear when you smear it with the heel of your hand going forward on the board. If it flakes or crumbles, add water, 1 tablespoon at a time, as needed.

Generously butter a large bowl and place the dough in it, rolling it around to butter the ball. Cover with a clean towel and let it rise in a warm, draft-free place until doubled in size, about 1 hour.

Punch down the dough and knead it again on the lightly floured board for a few minutes. Shape the dough into a loaf, folding two long sides of the bread toward each other, making a seam. Place the loaf, seam side down, in the prepared loaf pan. Brush with the egg wash and sprinkle with the 2 tablespoons sunflower seeds, pressing them into the top. Cover with a towel and allow the loaf to rise in a warm, draft-free place until the bread comes above the top of the pan, about 2 hours.

Preheat the oven to 350°F. Spray or brush the top of the loaf with cold water; bake until the top is nice and brown and the bread sounds hollow when you rap it with your knuckles, about 45 minutes. If the sides and bottom are not golden, take the bread out of the pan and bake on the rack 5 to 10 minutes longer.

GARDEN PEAS AND ORZO WITH FRESH MINT

Our peas are so sweet when we pick them that it's hard to get them from the garden to the table. We always start out with a big bowl, but no one can resist munching on the way back to the house. Orzo is a favorite pasta, about the same size as the peas. Our fresh mint begs to be picked because it grows in such profusion, and it's so special in combination with these two ingredients.

PHOTOGRAPH ON PAGE 137

SERVES 6 TO 8

1 cup orzo (rice-shape) pasta

2 cups water

1 teaspoon olive oil
   Kosher salt

3 cups shelled fresh peas

2 tablespoons butter, softened
   Freshly ground black pepper

1/2 cup chopped fresh mint

Combine the orzo, water, olive oil, and a pinch of salt in a medium saucepan. Cook over medium-low heat just as you would rice until the orzo is tender but not mushy, 12 to 15 minutes. Drain and set aside.

In another saucepan over medium heat, combine the peas and a pinch of salt with cold water to cover. Bring to a boil. Remove from the heat and let the peas sit for 10 to 15 minutes. Drain the peas in a colander and transfer to a large serving bowl. Add the cooked orzo and butter; toss to combine. Season to taste with salt and pepper, garnish with the fresh mint, and serve.

MEYER LEMON MERINGUE PIE

This is a family recipe from Tom's brother Mike, whose mission was to perfect their mother's lemon pie recipe. He has enhanced it by using his own homegrown Meyer lemons, which he brings to the ranch whenever he visits from California. Meyer lemons are full of juice and have thin skins. We always welcome his gift.

SERVES 8 TO 10

CRUST

1$^{1}/_{3}$ cups all-purpose flour

$^{1}/_{2}$ cup (1 stick) unsalted butter, cut into pieces

$^{1}/_{2}$ teaspoon kosher salt

2$^{1}/_{2}$ to 3$^{1}/_{2}$ teaspoons ice water

1 teaspoon cider vinegar

FILLING AND MERINGUE

1$^{1}/_{4}$ cups plus 6 tablespoons sugar

3 tablespoons cornstarch

1 tablespoon grated lemon zest

$^{1}/_{4}$ cup freshly squeezed lemon juice

3 large eggs, separated

1$^{1}/_{2}$ cups boiling water

Pinch of fresh cream of tartar (use jarred; without fresh, the egg whites will lack volume)

$^{1}/_{2}$ teaspoon pure vanilla extract

To make the crust: In the bowl of a food processor, combine the flour, butter, and salt. Pulse on and off until the mixture resembles coarse meal. Add a little ice water and the vinegar; pulse on and off, adding more water if necessary, until the dough comes together in a ball.

On a lightly floured surface, roll out the dough to an 11-inch round, $^{1}/_{4}$ inch thick. Transfer to a 9-inch pie plate and trim the edges, leaving the sides a bit taller than the plate to allow for shrinkage. Refrigerate for at least 30 minutes or overnight.

Preheat the oven to 425°F. Prick the bottom of the piecrust with a fork. Cut parchment paper to fit the bottom and up the sides of the pie shell. Line the pie shell and add pie weights or dried beans.

Bake for 20 minutes; remove the weights or beans and the parchment paper. Return the shell to the oven and bake, pricking down the crust if it puffs up, until lightly golden, 5 to 10 minutes longer. Let cool.

To make the filling: Combine the 1$^{1}/_{4}$ cups sugar, the cornstarch, lemon zest, and juice in a medium bowl. In a large bowl using an electric mixer on medium speed, beat the egg yolks; add the sugar mixture. Gradually add the boiling water and mix. Transfer the mixture to a medium saucepan. Bring to a boil over medium heat. Boil gently for 4 minutes, stirring constantly. Pour the filling into the cooled pie shell.

Preheat the oven to 425°F.

To make the meringue: In a medium bowl of a mixer on high, beat the egg whites. Add the cream of tartar when frothy. Gradually beat in the remaining 6 tablespoons sugar. Beat until stiff peaks form. Stir in the vanilla extract.

Spread the meringue on top of the pie all the way to the edge to seal in the filling. Bake until the meringue is browned, 4 to 5 minutes. Cool on a rack away from drafts.

NUMBER 307: PLAYING FAVORITES

MAKING NEW FRIENDS: *Ellen and her husband, Joe, meet one of the locals.*

OUR BISON HERD FEELS TO ME AS IF IT HAS ALWAYS BEEN ON this land, as it surely has. Surrounded by mountains, they roam over a thousand acres of a wide basin that's home to wildflowers and native grasses, as herds perhaps in the hundreds of thousands roamed hundreds of years ago. For the past eleven thousand years this land was essential in the lives of some four hundred generations of hunting and gathering peoples before they, along with their herds, were hunted to near-extinction. We need to pause often to remember that we are simply the stewards of this land. The real owners are the mulies and the white-tailed deer, the elk and the antelope, the bald and golden eagles and other raptors, and even the rattlesnakes, as they have been for centuries. And as I hope they will be for centuries to come.

We're among the few Montana ranches that still host a "domesticated" herd; at least some of our 150 herd wear ear tags, and we can easily identify the original 30 bred heifers that began our bunch. They live in fenced-off acreage, but they're anything but tame. Not much has been written about the family structure and hierarchy of the herds, but we've been gathering anecdotal information about those living on our land for some years now. The connections are fierce. The mothers and babies are distinct units and stay closely associated for several years; they seem to have the strongest ties. I've spent endless hours watching a cow direct her new calf and her yearling from the year before, spying on young calves cavorting with others, and marveling at huge bulls rolling in the wallows they've created. Family units are clearly defined; bison fathers play an active role in the herd during the rut (mating season) in late summer, but the rest of the year they more or less hang out together in bachelor

groups. When a bull is courting a female who has a baby and her yearling nearby, the yearling acts like a teenage babysitter and comes between the baby and the mother so that the mother can go off with the bull. The group of older bulls—four- to six-year-olds—are the players during this season, but females rule the rest of the time.

NEW KID ON THE BLOCK: *Bison mothers are extremely protective of their calves, which don't look anything like the behemoths they'll become.*

Gradually, you notice individuals. Bisons don't all look alike, and they have different personalities. Although they seem docile, they're definitely wild animals—it would be a mistake to wander among them, because their behavior is unpredictable. Yellowstone park rangers spend hours lecturing visitors and posting notices to warn them to keep their distance from the animals, but every summer seems to bring another report of a tourist foolishly trying to get an ever closer photo, only to be charged by an animal.

It's best to observe bison from the back of a pickup. As the vehicle moves slowly out into the pasture, the driver leans on the horn to attract the attention of the herd. They respond because by now they've learned that we'll be scattering pellets made from oats and molasses, which they apparently find irresistible. They've become acclimated to us in this way, and that makes it possible for us to watch them closely—so long as we have our pellet bribes.

One of the original females to arrive at our ranch is, from our human standpoint, a standout. She's number 307, and she'll thrust her black sandpaper tongue out to reach for a handheld nugget. She's the only one that will do this. Number 307 is our favorite.

STREAMSIDE SUPPER

COLD KIRS

FONTINA AND ASPARAGUS BRUSCHETTA

LEMON SALMON

WILD RICE PILAF

WATERCRESS SALAD

FOUR FAVORITE SALAD DRESSINGS

CUSTARD CUPS
WITH FRESHLY GRATED NUTMEG

COLD KIRS

As the sun is going down and the day cools, the Adirondack chairs down by the river call. A cold, crisp white wine with a splash of ruby cassis makes for the perfect summer drink.

SERVES 6

1 bottle Chardonnay, chilled

3 ounces (6 tablespoons) crème de cassis

Pour the wine into 6 pretty wineglass flutes. Add 1 tablespoon crème de cassis to each glass and stir. Serve cold.

FONTINA AND ASPARAGUS BRUSCHETTA

There are many ways to make bruschetta, but the most unusual one I know of combines a good slice of toasted country bread topped with fresh asparagus spears and aged Italian cheese and broiled to perfection. I think it could qualify as a grilled open-faced cheese sandwich, but because the toast is rubbed with garlic in the classic manner and the topping is vegetable, it falls into the ever-expanding bruschetta category. In any case, the combination of tastes works very well and pleases the eye as well as the palate.

SERVES 6 TO 8

1 loaf Italian peasant bread

Olive oil, for brushing

2 plump garlic cloves, peeled and halved

12 to 16 small to medium asparagus spears, trimmed (tips plus 4 inches)

1 cup grated Fontina cheese

3 tablespoons grated Parmesan cheese

Preheat the oven to 350°F.

Cut the bread on the diagonal into 1-inch-thick slices. Brush each slice lightly on both sides with olive oil. Place the slices on an ungreased cookie sheet. Bake the bread, turning once, until hard and golden, 6 to 8 minutes on each side.

Preheat the broiler.

Rub a cut side of garlic on one side of each slice and arrange the slices on the cookie sheet. Top each slice with 2 spears of asparagus.

In a small bowl, combine the Fontina and Parmesan cheeses. Sprinkle 2 tablespoons of the cheeses on top of each toast.

Broil the toasts 2 to 3 inches from the heat until the cheese is melted and bubbling. Serve immediately.

LEMON SALMON

1/4 cup olive oil

1 (4-pound) salmon side
with skin

2 lemons, sliced, plus
2 lemons, quartered
and seeded, for garnish

1 medium onion, sliced

1 bay leaf

6 peppercorns

1/4 cup half and half

1/4 cup chopped fresh parsley

When my two brothers and their families visit the ranch from their homes in Washington state, they bring us fresh Pacific wild salmon. This is always a highly anticipated get-together, and the salmon is never disappointing, especially to Montanans, who rarely get fresh fish like this. When it's cooked slowly, as it is in this recipe, the result is a moist lemony fish that is the Pacific wild salmon at its best.

SERVES 6 TO 8

Preheat the oven to 350°F or prepare the grill for a slow, steady fire.

Oil a piece of heavy-duty aluminum foil with about 1 teaspoon olive oil and lay it on a jelly-roll pan. Place the salmon on the foil, skin side down. Drizzle the remaining oil over the fish. Arrange the lemon slices, onion slices, bay leaf, and peppercorns on and around the fish, even underneath. Drizzle with the cream. Bring the long edges of the foil up on top of the fish and fold two or three times, leaving room for steam; fold the ends to seal the package.

Bake until the salmon flakes when a fork is turned in the flesh, 40 to 45 minutes. If grilling, place the package directly on the grill rack. Cook over indirect heat, with the grill covered, 40 to 45 minutes.

To serve, remove the skin and bay leaf and garnish with lemon quarters and chopped parsley.

WILD RICE PILAF

How can wild rice not be rice? But it isn't. It's a long-grain marsh grass now commercially grown in the Midwest. It's indigenous to the northern Great Lakes, especially Minnesota, where local American Indians have been harvesting it for years. Although it's expensive and takes about an hour to cook, its nutty and crunchy texture is well worth the effort.

2 cups wild rice

2 tablespoons butter

8 cups mild chicken stock

3 tablespoons dried currants

3 tablespoons toasted
pine nuts

SERVES 6 TO 8

Wash the rice several times in a sieve, then let it sit in cold water to allow any imperfect grains to come to the surface. Discard these unwanted grains and drain the rice.

Melt the butter in a large saucepan over medium heat. Add the rice and cook, stirring, until it changes color, about 7 minutes. Pour in the stock and bring to a boil. Reduce the heat, cover, and simmer until the grains of rice are tender but still crisp, about 1 hour.

Toss the rice in a serving bowl with the currants and pine nuts and serve.

WATERCRESS SALAD

I'm attempting to start some watercress in what should be a perfect sheltered spot on the bank of our river. Until it takes root, our source is the stream at the Heminways, our generous neighbors. There is nothing like the sweet and tender taste of freshly picked watercress, not to mention its high levels of vitamins, minerals, and phytochemicals.

SERVES 6 TO 8

2   bunches watercress

1   head endive

2   scallions

$^1/_2$ cup salad dressing
    (choose a favorite from
    those that follow)

Wash the watercress and trim off the large stems. Spin the leaves dry in a salad spinner and transfer to a large salad bowl. Wash and core the endive and separate the leaves. Cut them in quarters and add to the salad bowl. Clean and slice the scallions' white and green parts; add to the bowl. Cover the bowl and refrigerate until ready to serve. Toss the salad with the dressing just before serving.

FOUR FAVORITE SALAD DRESSINGS

These four dressings should be in everyone's repertoire. Make enough for several salads and keep it in a mason jar for easy use. Use within a week or so and you won't need to refrigerate.

CLASSIC VINAIGRETTE

$^3/_4$ cup olive oil

$^1/_4$ cup good-quality red wine
    vinegar

1   teaspoon dry mustard

1   teaspoon sugar

1   teaspoon kosher salt

2   medium garlic cloves,
    crushed through a press

MAKES 1 CUP

Place all the ingredients in a glass jar and shake well.

BALSAMIC VINAIGRETTE

³/₄ **cup olive oil**

2 **tablespoons balsamic vinegar**

1 **tablespoon good-quality red wine vinegar**

1 **teaspoon sugar**

1 **teaspoon kosher salt**

MAKES 1 CUP

Place all the ingredients in a glass jar and shake well.

RICE WINE VINAIGRETTE

³/₄ **cup olive oil**

3 **tablespoons rice wine vinegar**

1 **teaspoon dry mustard**

¹/₂ **teaspoon sugar**

¹/₂ **teaspoon kosher salt**

1 **large clove garlic, crushed through a press**

MAKES 1 CUP

Place all the ingredients in a glass jar and shake well.

BIG-BATCH SHALLOT VINAIGRETTE

3 **cups olive oil**

1 **cup good-quality red wine vinegar**

12 **shallots, finely chopped**

1 **teaspoon kosher salt or to taste**

1 **teaspoon freshly ground black pepper or to taste**

MAKES 4 CUPS

Place all the ingredients in a glass jar and shake well.

For a smaller batch, use ¹/₂ cup olive oil, 3 tablespoons vinegar, and 2 shallots.

CUSTARD CUPS WITH FRESHLY GRATED NUTMEG

Everyone seems to appreciate the silky-smooth texture of these little individual custards. If you provide a dish of whole nutmegs and a small grater at the table, guests can garnish their own custards.

SERVES 6 TO 8

3 cups milk

One 1-inch piece vanilla bean, split, or 2 teaspoons pure vanilla extract

4 large eggs

4 large egg yolks

$^1/_2$ cup sugar

1 nutmeg seed

1 cup cold heavy cream, for serving

Preheat the oven to 325°F.

Heat the milk and vanilla bean in a medium saucepan over medium heat until almost simmering (the milk should make a spitting noise when you tilt the pan). Remove the pan from the heat and remove the vanilla bean with a slotted spoon; scrape the small seeds from the bean into the milk. Discard the vanilla bean pod. If using vanilla extract, add it now.

In a large bowl with an electric mixer on medium speed, beat the eggs, egg yolks, and sugar together until they turn very pale yellow, 3 to 5 minutes. Slowly add a little of the hot milk to the egg mixture. Stir with a wooden spoon (see Note). Add the rest of the milk, stirring, in a thin steady stream. Strain the custard through a fine strainer and divide it evenly among 6 or 8 (8-ounce) custard cups.

Place the cups in a large roasting pan filled with 1 inch of hot water; this technique is called a bain-marie and cooks the custards slowly and evenly. Place the pan on the middle rack of the oven. Bake until the custards set, 50 to 60 minutes. Remove from the oven and let cool in the water bath. When cool, remove the cups from the water bath, cover, and refrigerate until ready to serve.

Grate fresh nutmeg over the custards before serving, or let your guests grate their own at the table. Serve with a pitcher of cold heavy cream.

NOTE: Bubbles ruin the texture of custard. You want no air bubbles when you add the milk to the egg mixture. This is the reason you switch from the electric mixer to a wooden spoon.

THE FISHERMAN GOURMAND

BY JIM HARRISON

I've always liked to present the image of a hearty fellow who wears rough-hewn clothes and drives a dirty SUV, hunts birds, and prefers fishing to all other activities. However, I've never cared for what is called camp food in the outdoor community. I recall an expedition to the borders of Yellowstone Park in the early 1970s with my friend Guy de la Valdene and a number of Livingston sportsmen. While the others were out for early-season elk, Guy and I fly-fished Suce Creek. It was visually interesting fishing because the others, who were on horseback, were trying to drive a herd of elk out of the park so they could be shot legally. This was a fresh insight into western life. However, dinner was something called Bob's Campfire Chili, a wretched potage of hamburger, chunks of tomato big as a baby fish, literally pounds of chopped celery, kidney beans, and scarcely any seasoning. We did fake eating like they do in the movies, pretended whiskey was food, and took over the cooking chores the next day.

A nutritional scholar studying northern Plains foodways would come up with a slender volume indeed. Fine cuisine assumes a certain amount of leisure and money. I'm not on a high horse; everyone gets to eat what they want. I didn't shrink back from the Nuts and Gizzards $3.95 special of deep-fried

calf testicles and chicken gizzards in the Sandhills of Nebraska, which were fine when covered by a pink sheen of Tabasco. This proves I'm a normal guy. In addition to having your own garden, the miracle of Montana food is offered by Federal Express and United Parcel Service. The world's food supplies are available on an overnight basis. Only moments ago, I opened a cooler containing three fresh abalone and some loins of albacore tuna sent by a predatory friend in California.

I'm lucky enough to work hard the rest of the year and fish for fifty to sixty days in the warmer months with my friend and guide Danny Lahren. We float the Big Hole, the Missouri, but mostly the Yellowstone. As others have noted, a life outdoors encourages the appetite. For coronary reasons I a void the classic Montana breakfast of side pork or chicken-fried steak with eggs, potatoes, and cream gravy, though I admit to loving it. I trade the rowing chores with Danny because I'm the usual neurotic writer and like the soothing, somewhat autistic rhythm of rowing. Also, you get to eat more with impunity.

But what to eat? When fishing the Big Hole or the Missouri, we detour to the Front Street Market in Butte, a very good delicatessen, and curiously the closest at hand. The owner, Jim Yakawich, prepares us a huge sandwich on ciabatta bread that includes provolone, mortadella, and salami. We add Italian vinaigrette, onion, and roasted peppers in the boat just before eating to avoid the sandwich becoming soggy—few sportsmen are hearty enough to eat a wet sandwich. If the weather is cool enough, we pack along a Côtes du Rhône for the late afternoon. Frankly, alcohol in more than scant amounts is counterindicated in fly-fishing. Leaders become tangled and fish are misstruck, so the wine is usually saved for the last half hour of the day's fishing.

For our Yellowstone floats I order supplies from Zingerman's in Ann Arbor, Michigan, arguably the best all-around delicatessen in America, with a grand array of the world's cheeses, especially French and English. Equally important are gift packages from the renowned chef Mario Batali in New York City and his father, Armandino, in Seattle. From this father and son pair I receive a dozen different artisanal salamis, lamb and duck prosciutto, as well as the sacred *guanciale* (treated pork cheeks) for the evening pasta course. There are also chunks of *lardo* taken from the neck fat of pigs fed only on milk and cream and fruit in the glorious last months of their lives, not less glorious than our own in my opinion.

Frankly, though, food is rarely on my mind during the hours of actual fishing, and my purge from the cultural detritus (a euphemism) that my profession often buries me in and that drives me to all the comparative solitude I can muster. Fishing requires a magnum level of attention that is curiously restorative rather than exhausting. We carry the new Sibley bird book and binoculars, and identifying birds is the only break in our concentration. We can chat about food, wine, or women but not about politics.

When our more exotic food supplies run short, we pick up fried chicken and coleslaw from Albertsons. Until lately, I'd scorned this fried chicken, but to my surprise have found it quite good. One must order the dark meat assortment, as wise heads have determined that the ubiquitous "skinless, boneless, chicken breasts" have sapped the moral vigor of America. Generally speaking, both the mammalian and the avian species are careful about what they eat. Junk food is junk, and you can't let down your guard when fishing.

BACK HOME ON THE RANGE

BUTTERFLIED TURKEY ON THE GRILL

COUNTRY-STYLE POTATO AND ONION PIE

ASPARAGUS WITH LEMON ZEST

FRIED GREEN TOMATOES

APPLE PANDOWDY

BUTTERFLIED TURKEY ON THE GRILL

1 (10- to 12-pound) turkey,
  butterflied (see Note)

1 cup freshly squeezed lime
  juice (from about 10 limes)

3 tablespoons dried oregano

1/2 cup (1 stick) butter, melted

  Kosher salt and freshly
  ground black pepper to taste

It doesn't have to be Thanksgiving or any other holiday for us to serve turkey for dinner. Cooked on the grill and seasoned with lime juice and oregano, the meat acquires a rich smoky flavor that's quite different from that of the oven-roasted variety. Since a ten-pound bird will serve a large group, this is a recipe that we rely on throughout the year. It's really easy, and the conventional cooking time is cut by a third.

SERVES 8 TO 10

Place the turkey, bone side down, in a large ceramic baking dish. Drench the bird with 1/2 cup lime juice. Sprinkle the oregano under the wings and a little over the rest of the turkey. Marinate for a few hours in the refrigerator.

Prepare a hot grill. Combine the melted butter and the remaining 1/2 cup lime juice and set aside.

Season the turkey with salt and pepper. Grill the bird, skin side up, over indirect heat with the grill covered, until a meat thermometer inserted in the thickest part registers 180°F, 60 to 90 minutes. Baste occasionally with the butter mixture and turn once near the end to crisp the skin.

NOTE: If I can get my butcher to butterfly the turkey, I let him; I prefer his job to mine. He splits the backbone down the middle and bends the bones so that the bird lies flat. The breast is in the middle with one leg and wing on either side, making a large flattened bird. Butterflying exposes the whole bird to the heat of the grill and promotes faster cooking.

COUNTRY-STYLE POTATO AND ONION PIE

1/4 cup (1/2 stick) butter

5 large new potatoes, sliced

2 medium onions, sliced

12 large eggs, lightly beaten

2 cups grated Swiss cheese

1/2 cup milk

1/2 cup chopped fresh parsley

1/2 teaspoon kosher salt

1/2 teaspoon freshly ground black pepper

We make this pie in a cast-iron skillet that travels from oven to table. This savory accompaniment of potatoes, onions, and melted cheese is perfect with chops, roasts, fish, or poultry. So are its many variations: crumbled browned sausages, scallions, chives, coriander, and different kinds of cheese.

SERVES 6 TO 8

Preheat the oven to 400°F.

In a 10-inch cast-iron skillet, melt the butter over medium heat. Add the potatoes and onions. Bake until they are tender and crispy, about 25 minutes.

In a medium bowl, combine the eggs, cheese, milk, parsley, salt, and pepper. Pour over the potato-onion mixture. Bake the pie until the eggs are set, 20 to 30 minutes longer.

GREEN WITH ENVY

HIGH-ALTITUDE GARDENING CAN BE CHALLENGING, TO SAY THE least. The season is short because temperatures often dip below freezing well into June, and frost can hit again by the end of August or the first of September. The obvious reality is that trying to grow tomatoes in a Montana vegetable garden is a fool's effort. Even so, my childhood memory (instilled at a lower altitude, in a zone or two farther south) of a freshly picked Big Boy warmed by the sun, lightly salted, and eaten like an apple, with the juice dripping down my chin, died hard. This was an essence of summer that I couldn't relinquish, so year after year I made the effort to grow tomatoes. It was always a race with the calendar, and rarely did the garden win, except for an occasional fluke. One year I heard about a type of Siberian tomato plant that promised a relatively short germination period, so it found its way into our patch. It grew. It ripened. It had no taste.

Now the garden is filled with lettuce, spinach, Swiss chard, peas, carrots, zucchini, and beets but, for the past several years, no tomatoes. Fortunately, the local farmers' market offers tomatoes (and more) from lower-altitude Montana gardens and farms, so I can at least have my summer tomatoes, even though I now admit I can't grow them. I should mention that one of our neighbors recently decided to plunge ahead with a tomato garden. She ignored the fact that most people think tomatoes are red and harvested her fruit in the green stage. She shared some of her crop with us, and we enjoyed fried green tomatoes and green tomato relish more than I thought possible. Now I'm rethinking the place of these plants in our garden. As long as we plan on picking them green, with no thoughts of another color, it should work. I can always sneak in the reds from the market.

In the space previously allotted to our moribund tomato plants, we've now switched to flowers, which flourish next to the vegetables that do thrive. Legend has it that gardens that mix veggies and annuals have a superior production; I think it's true: marigolds next to lettuce and spinach seem to ward off unwanted bugs; dahlias, sweet peas, snapdragons, sunflowers, zinnias, and hollyhocks seem now to belong together. The mix makes for a prettier garden, for one thing. Also it's more fun to harvest when you can do a vegetable here and a flower there, and cover the kitchen and the dining room all at once. And we just kind of slide in those perfect tomatoes from the market.

These chartreuse beauties look inviting, but they'll taste good only when cooked or left to turn red.

ASPARAGUS WITH LEMON ZEST

32 to 36 medium (index–finger-thick) asparagus stalks, trimmed of woody bottoms

$^1/_2$ cup Rice Wine Vinaigrette (page 152)

2 tablespoons lemon zest (from 2 lemons)

Our garden produces an abundance of asparagus from June to late July. Now that it's established, we even have stalks to give away. Asparagus steams quickly to perfection if you use a tall covered asparagus pot. You can also use a big frying pan with a lid—Ellen's favorite method. Lemon zest adds a pleasing crunch and wonderful flavor.

SERVES 8

Place the asparagus in a large skillet with cold water to cover. Cover and bring to a boil over medium-high heat. Reduce the heat and simmer until you can pierce the stem easily with a sharp knife, 10 to 13 minutes, depending on the thickness of the asparagus. Drain the asparagus and place on a platter.

Drizzle the vinaigrette over the warm asparagus and sprinkle with the zest. Serve hot or at room temperature.

FRIED GREEN TOMATOES

2 cups canola oil

1 cup white or yellow cornmeal

3 tablespoons all-purpose flour

$^1/_2$ teaspoon paprika

$^1/_2$ teaspoon garlic powder

$^1/_4$ teaspoon cayenne pepper

Kosher salt to taste

2 large eggs

4 large green tomatoes, cored and sliced $^1/_2$ inch thick

At the ranch's 5,500-foot altitude, we don't get red tomatoes because of the short growing season. But fully developed green tomatoes become quite acceptable for many dishes, this being a very good one. Quickly fried in a cornmeal batter, seasoned with garlic and pepper, they deserve much more respect than as a just-okay runner-up to their red cousins.

SERVES 6 TO 8

Heat the oil in a large heavy skillet over medium-high heat until it is hot but not smoking.

Meanwhile, combine the cornmeal, flour, paprika, garlic powder, cayenne pepper, and salt in a shallow bowl. Lightly beat the eggs in another shallow bowl. Dip each tomato slice in the egg and let the excess drip off. Dredge in the seasoned cornmeal, shaking off any excess. In small batches, carefully add the slices to the hot oil and fry, turning once, until browned, 2 to 3 minutes per side. Transfer to paper towels to drain. Serve immediately.

APPLE PANDOWDY

This dessert is made in a pie plate and topped with a nonfancy crust—some might even say that it lacks style. The topping looks like a primitive quilt made up of casually placed squares. An informal pie like this one can be a hit even with the fashionable eaters. The spices in the juice that the apples steep in also bathe the crust.

SERVES 8 TO 10

CRUST

- 1 cup all-purpose flour
- 10 tablespoons (1^1/$_4$ sticks) unsalted butter
- 3 tablespoons ice water

FILLING

- ^{3}/$_4$ cup firmly packed brown sugar
- ^{1}/$_2$ cup apple juice
- 2 tablespoons freshly squeezed lemon juice
- 1 teaspoon ground cinnamon
- ^{1}/$_2$ teaspoon ground ginger
- ^{1}/$_2$ teaspoon ground nutmeg
- ^{1}/$_8$ teaspoon ground cloves
- 8 large Granny Smith apples (about 4 pounds), peeled, cored, and sliced ^{1}/$_2$ inch thick
- 2 tablespoons unsalted butter
  Cold water, for brushing
- 1^1/$_2$ tablespoons granulated sugar
  Whipped cream or Homemade Vanilla Ice Cream (page 210), for serving

To make the crust: Pace the flour and butter in the bowl of a food processor. Pulse on and off until the dough resembles coarse meal, 5 to 6 times. Add the ice water and pulse briefly until the dough forms a ball. On a lightly floured surface, gently pat the dough into a flattened ball. Wrap in plastic and refrigerate for 30 minutes.

On a lightly floured surface, roll the dough to a ^{1}/$_4$-inch-thick rectangle, about 9 by 12 inches. Cut into about twelve 3-inch squares and transfer to a cookie sheet; cover lightly with plastic wrap or a thin clean towel. Refrigerate for at least 30 minutes or overnight.

Preheat the oven to 425°F. Butter a deep 12- by 10-inch baking dish (or similar size).

To make the filling: In a medium bowl, combine the brown sugar, apple juice, lemon juice, cinnamon, ginger, nutmeg, and cloves. Add the apples and toss to combine. Spoon the mixture into the baking dish and dot with the butter.

Arrange the chilled dough squares on top of the apples, overlapping them in a casual way. Brush the squares with cold water and sprinkle with the granulated sugar. Bake until the pandowdy starts to bubble and the crust is lightly browned, about 30 minutes. With a bulb baster, baste the crust with the juices from the bottom of the baking dish. Return the pandowdy to the oven and bake until the top is quite golden, about 30 minutes longer. Remove and let cool before serving with whipped cream or ice cream.

RODEO VITTLES

CHILLED BEET SOUP
WITH SOUR CREAM AND DILL

PARMESAN PAN BISCUITS

ELK PEPPER STEAKS

BOULDER RIVER BAKED BEANS

QUICK SNAP PEAS

RHUBARB CRISP

CHILLED BEET SOUP
WITH SOUR CREAM AND DILL

6 to 8 good-size beets
   (4 pounds)

6 cups strong chicken broth

$^1/_2$ cup sour cream, plus more
   for serving

1 medium cucumber

   Kosher salt and freshly
   ground white pepper to taste

3 large russet potatoes,
   peeled, cooked, and cut into
   medium dice, for serving

   Chopped fresh dill and/or
   chopped fresh chives,
   for serving

With all the beets we produce in summer, I make this soup and freeze tons of it, adding the sour cream when serving. We set out little bowls of cubed cooled potatoes, chopped dill, and chives and let our guests choose their favorites. When Ellen comes to visit, she calls this plain old borscht. Everyone has his or her own version: borscht with brisket, tomatoes, and boiled potatoes; borscht with cabbage; borscht with condiments such as cubed boiled potatoes, sour cream, chopped cucumbers, chopped dill and other herbs, or onions. We've grown to love this interpretation, hot or cold.

SERVES 6 TO 8

Place the beets in a large saucepan with enough water to cover by 2 inches. Bring to a boil over medium heat and cook, covered, until tender when pierced with a knife, 20 to 30 minutes. Drain. Stick a fork in the cut end of a beet and place under cool running water; with a sharp paring knife, scrape the skin away. Repeat with the remaining beets. Remove the beet greens and reserve them for another use.

Cut the beets into medium dice. Place half (about 2 cups) in the bowl of a food processor; puree until smooth. In a large bowl, combine the beet puree with the broth; stir in the remaining diced beets. Stir in the sour cream and season to taste with salt and pepper. Cover and refrigerate until serving.

An hour before serving, peel and seed the cucumbers, then finely chop or grate. Stir into the soup. To serve, ladle into chilled soup bowls and garnish with dollops of sour cream. Pass bowls of potato, dill, and chives at the table for guests to serve themselves.

PARMESAN PAN BISCUITS

1/3 cup (2/3 stick) butter, melted

1 1/4 cups all-purpose flour

2 tablespoons grated Parmesan cheese

1 tablespoon sugar

3 1/2 teaspoons baking powder

1 tablespoon chopped fresh parsley

1 teaspoon chopped fresh basil leaves

About 1 cup whole milk

West or East or Midwest, it's an indisputable fact that biscuits are too good to refuse. These bars—flaky dough with cheese and butter—are easy to make in a one pan–one step way. Buying top-quality Parmesan and grating it yourself will make a big difference in taste. This is a good recipe to have for lots of different occasions.

MAKES 12 BISCUITS

Preheat the oven to 400°F. Butter a 9-inch square baking dish.

In a medium bowl, combine the flour, cheese, sugar, baking powder, parsley, and basil with a fork, using a light touch. Stir in just enough milk to moisten and form a soft dough.

Turn the dough onto a lightly floured surface and lightly knead a few times until smooth. Roll into an 8- by 6-inch rectangle. Cut in twelve 4- by 1-inch strips.

Place each strip in baking dish, turning to coat with melted butter. Arrange the strips in two rows; bake until browned, 20 to 25 minutes.

PREGAME CONCENTRATION:

A cowboy deep in thought about
the upcoming competition.

THE MANE EVENT

"GIVE HIM A HAND, FOLKS, THAT'S ALL HE'S GONNA GET," THE arena announcer's voice booms at the crowd. It's a line that's often repeated as one hapless rodeo cowboy after another bites the dust, failing to stick to his mount for the requisite ten seconds.

The rodeo—the Event—is in town, and we've all gathered to watch barrel racing, broncobusting, and bull riding. Rodeos in the West are an important element of the cowboy culture and a popular form of entertainment. These contests where cowboys can show off their riding, roping, and wrestling skills with livestock started among trail drivers and ranch hands in the late 1800s. Since then, they've developed into a big-money professional sport for the best riders and ropers, and an irresistible weekend attraction for the working ranch hands and tourists of the modern West.

Throughout the summer amateur rodeos are as common in the small towns of cowboy country as Sunday baseball games are in the rest of the country. It's a rough and dangerous sport, but that's part of the appeal for the participants and the crowds. It's also a direct connection to the Old West, when every day was hard and the men and women who mastered it were tough and resourceful. It's still a rough life, but that doesn't deter these guys.

We go every summer. If the announcer is good, the show is entertaining. If not, you have to be a die-hard bucking bronc fan to stay with it, or just roll your eyes at the familiar bad jokes. But new production values have brought the rodeo into the new millennium. Last year, for example, an electronic screen with the names of the cowboys and a scoreboard for the events was added to the fairgrounds (along with lots and lots of rotating advertising), but the cobs of corn on sticks, the hot dogs, the cotton candy, and the spirit have remained the same. It's definitely a piece of unchanged Americana that has great nostalgic appeal.

A good stock of buckin' broncs makes it tough to stay on, and even tougher to stay in one piece, but the guys who do it love it and show up week after week for the thrill of sticking out a ten-second ride. The purses have gotten fatter, so prize money is a factor, but you sense that at least some of these characters might actually pay for the chance to ride.

MONTANA HIGH: *The eight-second thrill ride—if you can stay on that long.*

The West is rich with legendary rodeo men—and a few women—who provide a link to the old days of the romanticized wild frontier. Growing up in the 1950s in South Dakota, I knew that native son Casey Tibbs was widely regarded as America's best all-around cowboy, a Tiger Woods on a saddle bronc. He appeared on the cover of *Life* and dated movie stars. When he went to Hollywood as his riding days were winding down, we all thought he'd become the next Gary Cooper. That didn't happen, but his name is still revered in our home state fifty years later.

In the summer months, rodeos are staged nightly to entertain the tourists in popular destinations such as Cody and Jackson Hole, Wyoming, but the best may be the homegrown shows in the tiny towns deep in the heart of cow and horse country, like ours.

ELK PEPPER STEAKS

Legal hunting in Montana is what keeps our freezers stocked all year with elk, bison, venison, and antelope. The year-round residents on the ranch, Doug and Karen Campbell, hunt with traditional long bows, much the way the Crow Indians did on the same ground over the centuries.

Low in cholesterol and fat, these meats are very healthful, but because there's so little fat, they need a good marinade and a shorter cooking time than that required for beef.

SERVES 6 TO 8

$^1/_2$ cup soy sauce

$^1/_4$ cup olive oil

3 tablespoons honey

3 large garlic cloves, minced

1 tablespoon minced fresh ginger root

Juice of 2 limes

6 to 8 (6- to 8-ounce) elk, bison (see Selected Sources), or beef steaks

Coarsely ground black pepper

In a small bowl, whisk the soy sauce, olive oil, honey, garlic, ginger, and lime juice. Arrange the steaks in a large nonreactive pan, add the marinade, and distribute to evenly coat the steaks. Cover and refrigerate for 3 to 4 hours or overnight, turning the steaks once or twice.

About an hour before grilling, remove the steaks from the refrigerator and bring to room temperature.

Prepare a hot grill or preheat the broiler. Shake off an excess marinade and transfer the steaks to a plate.

Grind black pepper generously over each side of the steaks (about 2 teaspoons for each steak), pressing the pepper into the meat. Let the steaks rest at room temperature until broiling or grilling.

Grill or broil the steaks 3 to 4 inches from the heat, 3 to 4 minutes per side for medium rare. Let the steaks rest a minute or so before serving.

BOULDER RIVER BAKED BEANS

We've tried many baked bean recipes throughout our lives in Montana, New York, and elsewhere, but this one has a secret ingredient, thanks to a friend from Los Angeles: Roquefort cheese swirled in at the end of the cooking. It's a quirky addition that makes these baked beans stand out.

SERVES 6 TO 8

1 package (16 ounces) dried Great Northern beans, soaked in water overnight

3 strips bacon, cut into small strips

2 medium onions, chopped

2 garlic cloves, minced

³/₄ cup firmly packed dark brown sugar

¹/₂ cup apple cider vinegar

¹/₂ cup ketchup

¹/₄ cup molasses

1 tablespoon chili powder

1 teaspoon dry mustard (such as Colmans)

4 cups water, plus more if necessary

1 tablespoon Roquefort cheese Kosher salt to taste

Preheat the oven to 350°F.

Drain the beans.

In a 3-quart flameproof casserole over medium heat, cook the bacon until lightly browned. Add the onions and cook, stirring, until translucent, about 5 minutes. Add the garlic and cook a few more minutes. In a small bowl, combine the sugar, vinegar, ketchup, molasses, chili powder, and mustard; add to the casserole. Stir in the drained beans and water. Bring the mixture to a boil over medium-high heat.

Bake for at least 3 hours, testing and tasting toward the end and adding more water if the beans seem dry. The beans should be tender and the sauce should be the consistency of ketchup. Swirl in the Roquefort cheese at the end for the secret flavor. Season to taste with salt.

QUICK SNAP PEAS

The fresh snap peas that grow in our garden by the armful are another vegetable that barely makes it to my sink, because they're eaten on the way. Quickly sautéed in a little olive oil, they turn a luscious bright green, so they look lovely and still have that freshly picked taste.

SERVES 6

1 tablespoon extra-virgin olive oil

4 cups snap peas Kosher salt to taste

In a large nonstick skillet over medium-high heat, heat the oil until hot but not smoking. Add the snap peas and reduce the heat to medium. Cook, shaking the pan, until the peas turn bright green, about 3 minutes. Transfer the peas to a warm serving platter and sprinkle with salt. Serve immediately.

RHUBARB CRISP

FILLING

7 to 8 cups 1-inch pieces
   rhubarb (about 2 pounds)

2 cups sugar

2 tablespoons all-purpose
   flour

1 teaspoon grated lemon zest

TOPPING

$^1/_2$ cup (1 stick) plus
   2 tablespoons salted
   butter

1 cup firmly packed dark
   brown sugar

1 cup all-purpose flour

$^1/_2$ cup rolled oats

1 teaspoon ground cinnamon
   Pinch of kosher salt

Homemade Vanilla Ice
Cream (page 210) or
whipped cream, for serving

A rhubarb patch commands attention. Rhubarb is a beautiful bushy, broadleaf plant that grows like a weed, taking over more than its allotted space in the garden. Only the stalks are edible, and full of vitamin C, but that's all we need for this scrumptious dessert.

Warning: Freshly made warm rhubarb sauce is addictive, but overeating isn't recommended. Tom did so as a teenager, and all these years later he still can't look at rhubarb, however it's cooked.

SERVES 8

Preheat the oven to 375°F. Generously butter a 9- or 10-inch baking dish (square, round, or oval).

To make the filling: In a large bowl, combine the rhubarb, sugar, flour, and lemon zest; toss until combined. Transfer the mixture to the prepared dish.

To make the topping: In the bowl of a food processor, combine $^1/_2$ cup butter, the brown sugar, flour, oats, cinnamon, and salt; pulse on and off until the mixture resembles coarse meal. Crumble the topping evenly over the rhubarb. Dot with the remaining 2 tablespoons butter.

Bake on the middle rack until the top is browned and bubbly, about 30 minutes. Serve with ice cream or whipped cream.

THE BIG GRILL

NAN'S SUN-BREWED MINT ICED TEA

SMOKEY GRILLED VEGETABLES

CHIPOTLE CHICKEN

BAR-B-Q RIBS

ABSAROKA CORN PUDDING

BERRY COBBLER

NAN'S SUN-BREWED MINT ICED TEA

2 quarts water

12 to 16 whole fresh mint leaves, plus sprigs for garnish

6 to 7 tea bags of choice

Sugar to taste

Ice

Tea steeped in the sun is what I learned from my dear grandmother, Edythe Harvey, my "Nan." My mother and I lived with Nan and Gramp while my father was in the army during World War II. Nan grew up in the late 1800s and was probably following the simple traditions of pioneer women with this recipe—though in those days the tea was loose-leaf. Besides making a beautiful pitcher to look at, the tea meets all taste expectations: clear and mellow, with fresh mint to give it an extra sweetness on a hot summer day.

SERVES 8

Place the water and mint leaves in a large pitcher and hang the tea bags over the edge of the lip. Sweeten to your taste with the sugar. Cover the pitcher with plastic wrap and let the tea sit in the sun for a few hours. Serve in glasses with lots of ice and garnish with a sprig of mint.

SMOKEY GRILLED VEGETABLES

1/3 cup olive oil, flavored with a crushed garlic clove

4 ears corn, husked and halved

2 red, yellow, or green bell peppers, cored, seeded, and halved

1 eggplant, cored and sliced 1 inch thick

2 large sweet onions, sliced 1 inch thick

3 zucchini, sliced on the diagonal 1 inch thick

2 yellow crookneck squash, sliced 1 inch thick

Cherry tomatoes on a skewer, or halved tomatoes

Kosher salt and freshly ground black pepper

2 lemons, halved

Red pepper flakes (optional)

We rely on our garden vegetables all summer for zucchini, asparagus, eggplant, corn, and often peppers and several different kinds of squash. Basting the vegetables in good olive oil and cooking them on the grill brings out their distinctive flavors. For a nutty corn flavor with a slightly different texture, for example, we squeeze fresh lime juice over shucked ears before putting applewood and mesquite chips into the fire. They add a sweet, smokey flavor.

SERVES 6 TO 8

Prepare a medium-hot grill. Drizzle the vegetables with olive oil. Brush the grill with oil to prevent sticking.

Set the rack 3 to 4 inches above the heat. In batches, grill the vegetables until tender and browned on all sides. Turn the eggplant, onions, and squash early in the grilling and no more. Use a grill pan or basket (if desired) for delicate vegetables. Grill each vegetable until tender. The time will vary.

Sprinkle with salt and pepper and finish with a squeeze or two of lemon juice. Pass the red pepper flakes for those who like the heat.

CHIPOTLE CHICKEN

2 (7-ounce) cans chipotle chilies in adobo sauce

1 cup tomato sauce (jarred or canned is fine)

3 (4-pound) roasting chickens, cut into quarters

5 lemons, cut into quarters and seeded

This is a good recipe for a hot summer day because, oddly enough, spicy food brings down the temperature of the body—a lesson learned over the centuries by people in many hot-weather cultures. Chipotles are ripened smoked jalapeño peppers and can be very spicy, so judge carefully.

SERVES 10 TO 12

In a small bowl, combine the chipotles and their sauce with the tomato sauce. Generously rub the mixture on all sides of the chicken quarters to marinate. Cover and refrigerate until ready to use, at least 2 hours.

Prepare a hot grill. Grill the chicken 4 to 5 inches above direct heat, turning once or twice, until they are nicely browned and the pink is gone from the center of the meat. The breasts will cook in about 10 minutes; the dark meat will take about 8 minutes longer.

Sprinkle with lemon juice from 2 or 3 of the lemon quarters. Serve the remaining quarters for garnish with the chicken.

BIG SKY GATEWAY: *There's not much point in having doors here. This overhead log gate is a typical ranch entrance in these parts.*

WELCOME TO THE NEIGHBORHOOD

SHORTLY AFTER WE MOVED TO MONTANA, I READ *DANCING AT THE Rascal Fair,* a novel by a native son, Ivan Doig, about life at the beginning of the last century in Montana. The main characters were Scottish immigrants (like my Auld ancestors on my father's side) who embarked from Glasgow, found their way to Montana, and were trying to survive the harshness of their new surroundings. Doig's description of the climate, the remoteness, and the tenacity it took just to survive had a huge impact on me. I looked at the country with new understanding and appreciation.

While there are still enclaves of Scots in the state, most of our county, Sweetgrass, was settled by Norwegians. With or without ranching experience, they heard the siren call of the Homestead Act and headed west in a steady stream. Abraham Lincoln had signed the act into law in 1862, granting all heads of households age twenty-one and older the right to buy 160-acre parcels of land. At stake were 270 million acres, or 10 percent of the country's public land. The only requirement was that the settlers had to live on the land for five years—called "proving up"— before it was theirs. In some instances Easterners who wanted to own the land but didn't want to live on it hired others to do it for them. They became known as squatters, and that, in fact, was my great-grandmother's job. While her husband stayed on the Cherry Creek Reservation working for the government as an Indian agent, Martha Webster Harvey loaded up the horse-drawn buckboard with my grandfather, Guy, and his siblings, Mamie and Jim, and headed out to sit in a soddy—a log house with a sod roof—for her employer. They raised sheep and some cattle and cut the grass for hay where they could. The homesteaders worked unthinkably long hours, and even then not many of them made it. Of the two million who filed for claims during the 124-year period of the Homestead Act, less than half were successful. The rest moved on, abandoning everything they had created. Even now, you'll come across old log structures all over the state. Many are dilapidated; even so, to my mind they have a proud, even heroic quality about them. You can easily imagine the hopes around which they were built.

Terry Baird, the extraordinarily talented local builder who renovated our farmhouse kitchen, has rescued a number of these cabins, reconstituting them for modern life. For us, he dismantled a nineteenth-century one-room log house that he found twenty miles from our property, moved it, and reassembled it. He added a sleeping porch, a bathroom, an upstairs bedroom, a front porch, and an outdoor shower, all the while maintaining the integrity of the original structure. Guests staying in it report that they feel they've arrived on the frontier.

As we soon learned, the Boulder River area is inhabited by a mix of old-timers and newcomers. (Even after sixteen years, we are still newcomers; I think we always will be.) Mostly we coexist in harmony and, to my delight, that old/new barrier often comes down, with the happy result of some surprising new friendships.

Johnny Hoiland, for example, has lived in his place since he was born. His parents came from Norway and built their homestead right on the river across from Tom Hoiland, another recent arrival and the owner of our farmhouse. (According to Johnny, they weren't related and didn't speak.)

We first met Johnny over the fence. He always provides facts about all the families who have come and gone from the area, and he remembers the years of bad floods, severe droughts, and unusually frigid winters

BREAKING BREAD: *Neighbors and out-of-state friends gathering around a picnic table is a common sight.*

when the mercury stayed below zero for days on end. Another neighbor, the photographer Bruce Weber, "discovered" Johnny and featured him in a spread in Italian *Vogue;* since then, his leathery chiseled face, framed by a well-worn felt cowboy hat, has appeared in many commercials. Johnny's tractor, trucks, and hay bailer are all vintage pieces of farm machinery and they, too, have made their way into advertising videos.

Eddie and Karen Miller and their family were the first neighbors we met in Montana. During the course of reporting on the changing face of the West in the late eighties, Tom had been introduced to this multigenerational family who had lived here for many years. Although they came from Absaroka, which is a good eighty miles away, we managed to arrange get-togethers every summer.

Eddie, Karen, Ed's mother, Esther, and occasionally their son Matt, when he wasn't rodeoing, would arrive late in the afternoon, go for a ride or at least check out the horses, stay for dinner, then head home at dark. I was always careful to serve beef—usually steaks—because, like so many other cattle ranchers, that's all they eat. Eddie, in fact, claimed never to have tasted chicken in his life.

Often Johnny would come for dinner when the Millers were there. After our meat and potatoes, Johnny would produce his accordion and play for us. Esther and Johnny knew and loved the same vintage songs, mostly polkas, so he played, she sang, and, on those evenings so soon after our arrival, Tom and I began to really settle in.

The Montana ranchers whom we've met are self-contained, accomplished, no-nonsense, "can do" people. They have to be, given their isolation and the difficulty of living in this relatively remote, sometimes harsh climate. The transplants—meaning you weren't born there—have to like and appreciate these virtues or they don't stay.

Our neighbors Tom and Laurie McGuane have lived in Montana for thirty years (which, of course, makes them newcomers!), educated their children here, and worked the land raising alfalfa hay for their cattle and their horses. They also breed and train cutting horses, and both of them have championship ribbons, trophies, belt buckles, and saddles that prove just how good they are at riding. Tom may be nationally recognized as an author of *New Yorker* short stories and highly acclaimed books, both fiction and nonfiction, but in Montana he's known first as a horseman.

We introduced ourselves to the McGuanes shortly after our arrival, and they in turn introduced us to Nan Newton and her husband, the jazz composer and pianist Dave Grusin. The two Toms and Dave spend as much time as they can fly-fishing. The rivers, streams, and spring creeks are like magnets; maybe that's why so many artists and writers hooked on this sport choose to live in this area. Their work allows them the flexibility to write or paint and still hit the river in time for the caddis hatch. That's true for Jim Harrison, who writes for us about the food he eats while he's fishing but has yet to include that kind of information in any of his novels. It's clearly one of the reasons Russell Chatham, the nationally known landscape artist, lives here. It's also the draw for James Prosek, writer, illustrator, and authority on trout around the world who spends as much time as he can in the state. And true also for writer Verlyn Klinkenborg, who has bought land in western South Dakota on the Montana border.

We met the high-energy Hannibal and Julie Anderson through the McGuanes. They raise sheep and cattle on the same ranch Hannibal's father started in the 1940s. In addition, Hannibal is a school superintendent, Julie is a physician's assistant, and they're the parents of five children.

Julie is one of the Whistle Creek Women, the group of women friends with whom I ride, hike, canoe, and camp out. Initially, horses and hiking were the activities that pulled us together, but we soon found that our mutual interests included children, books, philosophy, a moderate amount of gossip, and good food. On our Whistle Creek Women Adventure Nights, Laurie adds her southern cooking expertise; we never would have known how important grits were to one's well-being without her. Julie likes to bake, and her banana bread is outstanding. Nan brings the wine. I'm the meat provider, and since we cook on a camp stove we grill marinated bison, elk, or antelope steaks.

Distances anywhere are relative. Traveling a few hours for a dinner date is something that might seem sheer lunacy in our urban life, but because Montana's population is so spread out and the state is so vast, it isn't uncommon here. I think of these treks we've made to be with our Montana friends, and they seem utterly worthwhile.

The Whistle Creek caucus (left to right): Meredith, Julie Anderson, Nan Newton, and Laurie McGuane.

BAR-B-Q SPARE RIBS

There's no need to look further for a recipe for ribs. This one passes the big test for me: ribs that are charred but tender and meaty, with just the right amount of crunch. A lot depends on the quality of the meat—not overly fatty—but much depends on the marinade and the grilling as well.

SERVES 6 TO 8

2 racks (5 to 6 pounds) pork spareribs

Kosher salt and freshly ground black pepper

$^1/_2$ cup ketchup

$^1/_2$ cup firmly packed brown sugar

$^1/_4$ cup olive oil

1 large onion, thinly sliced

4 garlic cloves, finely chopped

2 tablespoons freshly squeezed lemon juice

1 tablespoon dry mustard (such as Colman's)

1 tablespoon Worcestershire sauce

Tabasco sauce to taste

Generously rub the ribs with salt and pepper. In a shallow dish, combine the ketchup, brown sugar, olive oil, onion, and garlic. Mix with a fork until blended. Stir in the lemon juice, mustard, Worcestershire, and Tabasco. Set aside.

Prepare a ready-hot grill.

Place the ribs on the grill rack about 4 inches over direct heat and cook, turning once or twice, for 20 minutes.

Baste the ribs with the sauce. Continue grilling, turning and basting every 10 minutes or so, until the ribs are done, 40 to 50 minutes longer, depending on the thickness of the ribs. The ribs are done when they are brown outside and cooked inside—no pink.

ABSAROKA CORN PUDDING

This crunchy, creamy local corn pudding gets a flavor boost from mild green chiles. The good news is that it can also be made with leftover corn cut from the cob, or with frozen corn. The thing that sets the dish apart is its soufflélike quality, which is sure to knock the socks off the company when it's presented. There's some confusion about the pronunciation of Absaroka: Ab-sa-ro-ka? Ab-sorka? Ab-sa-orka? There's no confusion about the demand for the pudding, though. It's just that good.

SERVES 6 TO 8

4 cups corn kernels (from about 8 ears), or 2 (10-ounce) packages frozen corn

³/₄ cup (1¹/₂ sticks) butter, melted

3 large eggs, separated

1¹/₂ cups sour cream

1¹/₂ cups grated Jack cheese

³/₄ cup yellow cornmeal

1 (4-ounce) can green chiles, drained and cut into ¹/₂-inch-wide strips

2 garlic cloves, chopped

Kosher salt and freshly ground black pepper to taste

Preheat the oven to 375°F. Butter a 3-quart soufflé dish or baking dish.

In the bowl of a food processor, combine 2 cups corn and the melted butter. Pulse on and off until well mixed. Transfer to a large bowl and add the egg yolks and sour cream; combine well. Fold in the remaining 2 cups corn.

In a medium bowl, combine the cheese, cornmeal, chiles, and garlic and season to taste with salt and pepper. Stir the cheese mixture into the corn mixture until blended.

In another medium bowl, beat the egg whites with an electric mixer on high speed until stiff peaks form. Fold the egg whites into the corn pudding mixture.

Spoon the mixture into the prepared dish.

Bake the soufflé until golden brown, about 1 hour. Serve immediately.

BERRY COBBLER

6 to 7 cups berries
(blackberries, huckleberries,
raspberries, or blueberries,
or a mixture; wash only
blueberries)

2 cups all-purpose flour

2 cups sugar

1 cup canola oil

1$^{1}/_{2}$ teaspoons baking powder
(check date on label to make
sure it is fresh)

$^{1}/_{2}$ teaspoon salt

Blueberries, huckleberries, raspberries, blackberries, or any combination are good. We prefer locally grown huckleberries when we can get them, but the huckleberry-obsessed pickers make it tough to find undiscovered berry bushes. Montana's commercial jam businesses have a corner on the market in some areas, and because the season is a brief couple of weeks in early August, it's a mad scramble.

This dough can be made in advance and placed in soft clumps on top of the berries before baking. It's especially good with Homemade Vanilla Ice Cream (page 210) or cold heavy cream, whipped or poured from a pitcher.

SERVES 8

Preheat the oven to 350°F.

Butter a deep 10- by 12-inch baking dish (or similar size) and add the berries.

In a large bowl, combine the flour, sugar, oil, baking powder, and salt with a fork. With your fingers, gather up clumps of the dough, about the size of lemons, and place on top of the berries. The dough will have small spaces in between the clumps for steam to escape as the cobbler bakes.

Bake the cobbler until the top is lightly browned, 30 to 40 minutes.

DINNER ON THE BRIDGE

EASY ROQUEFORT PINWHEELS

SORREL SOUP

FRESH HAM WITH 1,000 CLOVES OF GARLIC

McLEOD HOT MUSTARD

SKILLET BRANDIED SWEET POTATOES

GARDEN-FRESH SNOW PEAS

COLD GRAPEFRUIT SOUFFLÉ
WITH PISTACHIOS

FRESH HAM WITH 1,000 CLOVES OF GARLIC

The name of this recipe is a slight exaggeration, but you'll probably use more garlic cloves than you've ever used in one recipe before. (Don't worry—the roasted garlic has a mild taste.) This dish originates in the south of Spain and uses a fresh ham that's a whole leg of pork, not cured. It's juicy and tender and has a crispy, crunchy skin called crackling. It's a good big-party recipe, but it takes almost eight hours to cook, so give yourself plenty of time.

SERVES 18 TO 20

¼ cup vegetable oil

1 (2-inch) piece fresh ginger, peeled and grated (1 to 2 tablespoons)

1 tablespoon soy sauce

1 (16-pound) whole fresh ham, scored

3 garlic heads, broken apart, cloves unpeeled

3 tablespoons sherry or applejack brandy

2 cups beef broth (bouillon cubes or canned is fine)

2 tablespoons butter, softened

3 tablespoons all-purpose flour

Kosher salt and freshly ground black pepper

Preheat the oven to 300°F.

In a small bowl, combine the oil, ginger, and soy sauce; rub the paste all over the ham. Place the ham on a rack in a large roasting pan. Place 3 or 4 large garlic cloves in the pan and place the pan on the bottom rack in the oven. Roast 5 hours; discard the garlic. Add the remaining unpeeled garlic cloves. Continue roasting until an instant-read thermometer inserted deep into the ham registers 160°F, 1 to 2 hours longer.

Transfer the ham to a large platter and let rest for 15 minutes. Reserve the garlic cloves.

To make the gravy: Discard all but 1 tablespoon fat from the pan. Place the pan over medium heat and add the sherry or brandy, scraping the brown bits from the bottom of the pan. Stir in the broth and bring to a simmer. With a fork, mash the butter and flour into a paste—a beurre manie. Whisk the paste into the gravy; continue whisking until thickened. Season to taste with salt and pepper. Strain the gravy through a fine-mesh sieve and keep warm.

To serve, cut the ham into slices. Serve each portion with some crackling, a few garlic cloves, and a ladle of gravy.

AL FRESCO DINING

OUR NEIGHBORS NAN AND DAVE GRUSIN HAVE DISCOVERED AN ideal spot for their annual July dinner party. Some years ago, on an evening when their house hadn't recovered from the hot afternoon as it usually did, they hastily moved their tables down to the coolness of the riverbank, and thus began a tradition. The river runs through the middle of their ranch, and the bridge over it is right behind the barn, about fifty yards from the house. With its sturdy wooden slats, it makes for an extraordinary dining room. If the elements cooperate, the al fresco dining is just about perfect: no wind, few bugs, just soft light shining through the trees and glistening off the water. The river is a constant presence, almost like another guest.

The party usually begins at about seven, so there is plenty of daylight left. Because Montana is on such a northern latitude, darkness doesn't fall until almost 10:00 P.M. during June and between 9:00 and 9:30 in July and August. Nan has candles and lanterns ready for the tables as the sun sets, though, and the ambience continues. It does get chilly in this high elevation—we're at about 5,500 feet—so everyone knows to bring a sweater. (Nan is prepared with shawls and jackets for anyone who forgets.)

Everyone dresses up a bit, Montana style. That means putting on a broomstick skirt instead of the usual Wrangler jeans and your pointy cowboy boots instead of crepe-soled ropers. I've noticed that guys go for the elegant leathers, whereas fancy boots for women involve leather appliqués in contrasting colors. Nan's favorites are a pair of very chic red boots with subtle green threads running up and down the sides like scrambling vines in a Wild West garden. Laurie McGuane has hers handmade, a luxury.

Only a few finishing touches are necessary to complete this magical setting. Nan and caterer Susan Pauli add vintage chairs and tablecloths, buckets of wildflowers, and a collection of red lanterns with votive candles to complement the dappled light as the sun finally goes down. The sound of the river is accompanied by the chirps of the tree swallows out gathering insects, and by the occasional punctuating screech of a red-tailed hawk overhead. It's an evening that I look forward to each year.

You can almost hear the musical accompaniment of the river in this idyllic party scene.

McLEOD HOT MUSTARD

Hands down, this is the best homemade mustard in the world. It keeps for several months in the fridge and is excellent with steaks and chops, chicken and roasts, sandwiches and hot dogs. I'm never without it.

MAKES 3 CUPS

1 (4-ounce) container dry mustard (Colman's is a good choice)

1 cup cider vinegar

1 cup sugar

3 large eggs

In a large heavy-bottomed casserole over medium heat, combine the mustard and vinegar until blended. Add the sugar and eggs and cook, stirring with a wooden spoon, until the mustard thickens to the consistency of ketchup, about 7 minutes. Cool; store in a glass jar with a tight-fitting lid.

SKILLET BRANDIED SWEET POTATOES

This is one of those sweet potato dishes that can be popped into the oven with no mess or trouble when it's time to make dinner. Ellen discovered the combination of the potatoes and brandy when she first started cooking in California; the ingredients were in a soufflé, but the concept translated beautifully to this dish.

SERVES 6 TO 8

1 lemon, halved

6 large sweet potatoes

6 tablespoons (³/₄ stick) butter, cut into pieces

¹/₄ cup sunflower seeds, toasted

2 tablespoons brandy

Kosher salt and freshly ground black pepper to taste

3 tablespoons chopped fresh parsley, for garnish

Preheat the oven to 350°F. Butter a 9-inch cast-iron skillet.

Squeeze the juice from the lemon into a bowl of cold water.

Peel the sweet potatoes and slice ¹/₂ inch thick, dropping the slices into the lemon water to keep them from turning brown.

Dry the sweet potatoes. Layer them in the prepared skillet, dotting each layer with the butter and sprinkling with the sunflower seeds, brandy, salt, and pepper.

Bake the sweet potatoes, tightly covered with foil, 45 minutes. Remove the foil and bake until crisp and brown, 15 minutes longer.

To serve, invert on a platter and sprinkle with the parsley.

GARDEN-FRESH SNOW PEAS

We plant snow peas in the spring and harvest them well into the summer. They grow plentifully and will add a tasty crunch to just about anything.

4 **cups snow peas**

2 **tablespoons olive oil**

Pinch of kosher salt

SERVES 6

Wash the snow peas and remove any tough strings.

    Heat the olive oil in a large nonstick skillet over medium-high heat until hot but not smoking. Add the snow peas and reduce the heat to medium. Cook, shaking the pan, until the peas turn bright green, about 3 minutes. Transfer the peas to a warm serving platter and sprinkle with salt. Serve immediately.

COLD GRAPEFRUIT SOUFFLÉ WITH PISTACHIOS

The tartness of grapefruit is a wonderful departure from the typical lemon desserts. When you need a light and fresh, citrusy and crunchy dessert to finish a rich dinner, this is it.

SERVES 6 TO 8

1 teaspoon grated grapefruit zest, or lemon zest

1 cup strained fresh grapefruit juice (from 1 medium grapefruit)

2 teaspoons (1 package) unflavored gelatin

6 large eggs, separated (reserve 1 yolk for another use)

³/₄ cup sugar

1 cup milk

³/₄ cup heavy cream

¹/₄ cup chopped pistachios (without skins)

Select eight 4-ounce glasses with vertical (not sloping) sides. Cut 8 pieces of parchment paper or aluminum foil about 4 inches wide and long enough to wrap around the glasses and overlap. Wrap the paper around the glasses, extending above the tops by 2 inches. Secure with rubber bands or strings.

Combine the grapefruit zest and juice in a small bowl and sprinkle the gelatin on top. Set aside. With a fork, lightly whisk 5 egg yolks and ¹/₂ cup sugar in a medium mixing bowl. (Discard the remaining yolk or reserve for another use.)

Heat the milk in a medium saucepan over medium heat until almost simmering. The milk should make a spitting sound when you tilt the pan. Remove from the heat. Whisk about ¹/₄ cup hot milk into the egg-yolk mixture. A little at a time, whisk the egg-yolk mixture back into the hot milk in the pan. Cook over low heat, stirring constantly, until the mixture starts to thicken, about 5 minutes. Remove from the heat and stir in the gelatin mixture. Transfer to a large bowl and cool to room temperature.

In a clean bowl using an electric mixer, beat the egg whites on high speed until bubbles form. Add the remaining ¹/₄ cup sugar, slowly beating on high speed until stiff peaks form. Fold the beaten whites into the cooled custard.

In another clean bowl, whip the cream until the consistency of sour cream. Gently fold into the custard mixture.

Divide the mixture among the glasses, filling to the tops of the collars. Level off. Refrigerate until the soufflés are set, at least 6 hours or overnight. Before serving, remove the collars and gently press the pistachios, one handful at a time, onto the exposed sides of the soufflés. Or, if you don't want to use the collar, fill the glasses (or cups) and sprinkle the top with the chopped nuts.

GUESS WHO'S COMING TO DINNER

SESAME THINS

NOODLE POPOVERS

GRILLED LAMB
WITH CHIMICHURRI SAUCE

CARAMELIZED CARROTS

OLD-FASHIONED PEACH PIE

HOMEMADE VANILLA ICE CREAM

SESAME THINS

We freeze these thin wafers whenever I make them because they're nice to have on hand for a good nibble before dinner or even with a salad or a drink. The dough is easy to make in a food processor, and the wafers keep very well in a tightly wrapped tin. Life is too busy these days for most of us not to think to plan ahead this way.

MAKES 30 TO 36 COOKIES

$1/3$ cup sesame seeds

1 cup all-purpose flour

3 tablespoons vegetable shortening

$1/4$ teaspoon baking powder

Pinch of kosher salt, plus more for sprinkling

$1/4$ cup light cream

Coarse salt, caraway seeds, poppy seeds, sesame seeds, cumin seeds, or other topping of your choice

Preheat the oven to 350°F.

Place the sesame seeds on a cookie sheet and toast in the oven until golden brown, 15 to 20 minutes. Transfer the seeds to a heatproof bowl. Let cool. Set aside until ready to use.

Combine the flour, shortening, baking powder, and salt in the bowl of a food processor. Pulse on and off until the dough resembles coarse meal. Add the toasted sesame seeds; slowly pour in the cream while pulsing on and off; pulse until the mixture forms a soft ball. Turn the dough out on a lightly floured sheet of waxed paper. Cover with another sheet of waxed paper and roll the dough to an $1/8$-inch thickness. Chill for 1 hour.

Preheat the oven to 350°F. Grease a cookie sheet.

Remove the dough from the refrigerator and peel off the top sheet of waxed paper. Cut out rounds of dough with a 3-inch biscuit or cookie cutter. Place the rounds $1/2$ inch apart on the prepared cookie sheet. Bake on the center rack until golden brown, 15 to 20 minutes. Remove from the oven and sprinkle with a topping of your choice. Serve warm.

NOODLE POPOVERS

Popovers are impressive to look at—tall and elegant golden brown, with a crispy crust on the outside and creamy on the inside. And these taste even better. Guests will love them. If you don't have a popover pan, you can use a muffin tin.

MAKES 12 TO 16 POPOVERS

1 pint (16 ounces) sour cream

1/2 cup (1 stick) butter, melted, plus 1 tablespoon butter, softened

3 ounces cream cheese, softened

3 large eggs

2 teaspoons sugar

1 teaspoon freshly squeezed lemon juice

1 (16-ounce) package broad egg noodles

1/3 cup white raisins (optional)

In a medium bowl, combine the sour cream, melted butter, cream cheese, eggs, sugar, and lemon juice; whisk lightly with a fork. Cover and refrigerate overnight if possible.

Cook the noodles in a large pot of salted boiling water until al dente, a little chewy (add a little oil to the water, if you like). Drain and toss with the 1 tablespoon softened butter. Cover and refrigerate overnight if desired.

Preheat the oven to 350°F. Generously butter the cups of a 12-cup popover pan; set aside.

Fold the noodles into the cold egg mixture and combine well. Fold in the raisins, if using. Fill the popover cups two-thirds full with the noodle mixture. Bake until golden brown, about 45 minutes. Serve the popovers hot.

GRILLED LAMB WITH CHIMICHURRI SAUCE

1 (4-pound) boned and
butterflied leg of lamb

Chimichurri Sauce
(recipe follows)

Chimichurri sauce traveled everywhere with the gauchos—cowboys—of Chile and Argentina as they rode the fences for weeks at a time, living off lamb and wild rhubarb and whatever greens they could find. Our neighbors Yvon and Malinda Chouinard, who entertain large numbers of unexpected guests at the drop of a hat, brought this recipe back from one of their many trips to Patagonia.

Chile peppers in Argentina are very mild and soft. If you use Italian, Mexican, or American red pepper in this dish, just put in a pinch and taste. The sauce is not supposed to be hot but, rather, more tangy and interesting.

SERVES 8 TO 10

Place the lamb in a large nonreactive pan. Add about 1 cup sauce and turn the lamb to coat. Cover and refrigerate, turning the lamb a few times, at least 2 hours or overnight.

Prepare a hot grill.

Remove the lamb from the marinade. Place the lamb on the grill rack 4 inches over direct heat. Cover for about 5 minutes, then uncover. Continue grilling, turning once, until browned on the outside but still light pink on the inside, 20 to 30 minutes. Transfer the lamb to a cutting board. Let it rest for 10 to 15 minutes before slicing against the grain.

CHIMICHURRI SAUCE

1 cup olive oil

1 cup dried oregano

1 cup minced garlic

1 tablespoon dried crushed
red pepper flakes

1 teaspoon kosher salt

About 1 cup red wine
vinegar

This thick herb sauce is as common in Argentina as ketchup is in the United States. Chimichurri is a combination of olive oil, vinegar, and finely chopped herbs and seasonings. It has its roots in gaucho country with the cowboys who carried this sauce with them to season their meat before and after grilling.

MAKES ABOUT 3 1/2 CUPS

Put the olive oil, oregano, garlic, red pepper, and salt in a wine bottle. Add enough vinegar to fill the bottle, cover, and shake well.

NOTE: You can add more vinegar once or twice, as long as the spices hold up. Substitute dried basil for the oregano and feel free to add more garlic if you wish.

Make holes in the cork if you can, or simply sprinkle the sauce on your food as they did in the old days, or keep it in a cruet.

HOMEMADE VANILLA ICE CREAM

2 cups milk

³/₄ cup heavy cream

1 vanilla bean, split
   lengthwise, or 1 tablespoon
   pure vanilla extract

3 large egg yolks

¹/₂ cup plus 1 tablespoon sugar

Unless you have an old-fashioned crank machine and plenty of rock salt on hand, I recommend making homemade ice cream with an electric machine. The end product is just as good, whether it's served alone or as a topping for pies, crisps, brownies, or cobblers.

SERVES 6

In a medium saucepan over medium heat, bring the milk, cream, and vanilla bean, if using, to a boil. Remove the pan from the heat and remove the vanilla bean with a slotted spoon; scrape the small seeds from the bean into the milk mixture. Discard the brown pod.

In a large bowl, using an electric mixer on high speed, beat the egg yolks and all the sugar until pale yellow. Ladle ¹/₂ cup of the hot milk mixture into the yolk mixture and stir with a wooden spoon. Stir another ¹/₂ cup milk mixture into the yolk mixture. Then stir the yolk mixture into the hot milk. Bring to a simmer over medium heat. Remove from the heat. If using vanilla extract, stir it in at this point. Let the mixture cool. Freeze in an ice cream maker as directed by the manufacturer.

Old-fashioned Peach Pie (page 209)

with a scoop of vanilla ice cream

riding the open range had to make do with beans, beans, and more beans, townsfolk had enjoyed finer fare almost from the very first. The cattle barons frequenting the Cheyenne Club in the Wyoming Territory ordered eels, imported caviar, and the finest Roquefort cheese. An Odd Fellows dinner at the Drovers' Cottage in Abilene, Kansas, in 1871 (only four years after the first cattle pens were built there on the Union Pacific line) served pigeon pie, escalloped oysters, larded woodcock, blanc mange, and strawberry ice cream, along with dozens of other choices. Ten years later, a banquet for the Society of Colorado Pioneers at silver king T. A. Tabor's brand-new Windsor Hotel in Denver featured, among its many offerings, mock turtle soup, glazed sweetbreads with French peas, larded roast quail, roast beef with Yorkshire pudding, port wine jelly, and Neapolitan ice cream. I suppose I might have traveled down to Denver that summer in search of more interesting food, but I doubt I would have found a finer meal than the one stewed at the Windsor in 1881.

After thirty-five years in Montana, it's a whole new cup of stew. Grizzly bears, elk, and cougars still roam the surrounding mountains, but down in town things aren't quite the same. Gourmet restaurants are numerous now. You can get a latte at drive-through coffee stands in tiny communities out in the middle of nowhere. Although there's no shortage of chicken-fried steak, I recently feasted on grilled shad roe wrapped in pancetta at Chatham's Livingston Bar & Grill. Where once a grocery clerk greeted my request for capers with a quizzical "Capers?" there is now a live lobster tank in the local Albertsons. I view this not as progress but as a return to the more exacting standards of early times, an era that is ever receding into the realms of myth.

ACKNOWLEDGMENTS

Some of our generous neighbors have contributed their thoughts on Montana life.

Tom McGuane is a legendary horseman who's in the National Horse Cutting Association Hall of Fame. His love for the horse is inspiring. He irrigates his land to support the cattle he raises—that is, when he's not riding in cutting horse events or writing best-selling novels, short stories, and screenplays.

Jim Harrison's descriptive eye amazes and amuses all fans of his novels and short stories. He's also a world-class fisherman with some pretty definite ideas about what to eat while fishing.

William Hjortsberg, known throughout our part of the state as "Gatz," has spent years writing screenplays, novels, and magazine articles. Inspired by his restaurateur father, he's been fascinated with the history of food in the West and may be one of the few who has studied Montana cuisine styles.

James Prosek, whose trout paintings moved one critic to call him "the Audubon of the fish world," is also an avid fly fisherman and acclaimed author. He's currently working on a history of trout around the world.

Although he lives in the East, writer **Verlyn Klinkenborg,** one of America's most gifted nature essayists, frequently visits Montana and Wyoming, where he gathers material for his insightful pieces on the American West on the editorial pages of *The New York Times*.

Neighbor **Tom Murphy** is one of Montana's finest landscape and wildlife photographers, capturing the essence of life in one of the most glorious states in the union. His *Silence and Solitude* and T*he Light of Spring* are considered classic photographic descriptions of Yellowstone Park.

Through his camera lens, acclaimed food photographer **Tom Eckerle** inspires all cooks and would-be cooks. His food photography elevates food to works of art.

SELECTED SOURCES

Fresh bison meat, including shanks and ground, can be ordered online at www.buckfarmbison.com and www.kcbuffalo.com.

Chokecherry jams and syrups are available online at www.juniper-ridge.com. I don't think you can buy "fresh" chokecherries because they can't be refrigerated as other fruits can—they go bad. So if you come across a chokeberry bush where you live, cook the berries or eat them as soon as you pick them.

JustCorn is available at www.justtomatoes and at many specialty markets and health food stores.

INDEX

Page numbers in *italics* refer to illustrations.

chokecherry, 126, *126*
    glaze, pork tenderloin with, 123
    jelly, 125, *126*
    products, source for, 217
Chouinard, Malinda, 207
Chouinard, Yvon, 50, 51, 207
cilantro, 64
    in Running-W-Bar guacamole, 94
    slaw, 64
    in spicy tomato soup, 80
cinnamon rolls, Val's, 30, *32*, 33
cold grapefruit soufflé with pistachios,
    201
cookies:
    brown sugar–chocolate chip, 47
    icebox sugar, 82, *83*
corn:
    bread, jalapeño, 70
    dried roasted, in Stetson salad, 79
    pudding, Absaroka, 187
    in smokey grilled vegetables, 180
Coulter, John, 117
country-style potato and onion pie, 159
cowboys, 170–71, *170, 171,* 207, 213–14
Cow Camp, 55–65, *56*
cranberry and pear relish, 107
cream, custard cups with freshly grated
    nutmeg and, 153
cream, whipped:
    apple pandowdy with, 164
    burnt-sugar pumpkin pie with, 115
    gingerbread with, 107
    pear tatin with, 131
    rhubarb crisp with, 175
    in strawberry fool, 81
crème de cassis, in cold kirs, 146
croutons, Gorgonzola, 68
Crow Indians, 18–19, 58, 172
cucumber(s):
    in chilled beet soup with sour
        cream and dill, 168
    in cilantro slaw, 64
    in Grandma Jean's easy bread-and-
        butter pickles, 62
cupcakes, chocolate buttermilk, 72
curried chicken salad, 46
custard cups with freshly grated
    nutmeg, 153

D

Dancing at the Rascal Fair (Doig), 182
David (head cowboy), 53

Davis, C., 213
Denver, Colo., 214
desserts:
    apple pandowdy, 164
    berry cobbler, 188
    chocolate buttermilk cupcakes,
        72
    cold grapefruit soufflé with
        pistachios, 201
    custard cups with freshly grated
        nutmeg, 153
    fudgy brownies, 65
    gingerbread with whipped cream,
        107
    rhubarb crisp, 175
    strawberry fool, 81
    see also cookies; pies, dessert
dill, chilled beet soup with sour cream
    and, 168
Doig, Ivan, 182
Doyle, T., 213
dressing, salad, Stetson, 79
    see also vinaigrette
Drovers' Cottage, 214
Dutch oven(s), 114
    short ribs, 114

E

egg(s), 13, 22, *40*, 43
    and bacon pie, 26
    frontier, 43
    hard-boiled, spinach salad with
        bacon twists and, 68
eggplant, in smokey grilled vegetables,
    180
elk, 51, 61
elk pepper steak(s), 172
    with pepper and onion marmalade,
        46
endive:
    and beet salad, 112
    and watercress salad, 150

F

farmers' markets, 19, 160
feta (cheese):
    in chiles rellenos, 91
    and watermelon salad, 64
fish:
    lemon salmon, 148
    smoked trout with horseradish
        sauce, 36

fishing, 23, 50–53, *50, 51,* 185
    food supplies for, 154–55
flowers:
    in vegetable gardens, 161
    see also wildflowers
Fontina and asparagus bruschetta, 146
freeze-dried food, 50, 51
fried green tomatoes, 163
frontier eggs, 43
Front Street Market, 154–55
frosting, chocolate, 72
fruit, dried:
    in grange granola, 26
    see also apricots, dried; raisins
Fryer, John, 52
fudgy brownies, 65

G

garlic:
    Fontina and asparagus bruschetta
        with, 146
    fresh ham with 1,000 cloves of, 195
    sautéed Swiss chard with, 36
ginger:
    in fresh ham with 1,000 cloves of
        garlic, 195
    in marinade for elk pepper steaks,
        172
    and orange peel, candied, 49
gingerbread with whipped cream, 107
goat cheese:
    in bacon and egg pie, 26
    savory phyllo squares with sage
        and, 122
Gorgonzola croutons, 68
Grandma Jean's easy bread-and-butter
    pickles, 62
granola, grange, 26
grapefruit soufflé with pistachios, cold,
    201
Grill, The, 213
grilled:
    butterflied turkey, 158
    lamb with chimichurri sauce, 207
    vegetables, smokey, 180
grits, Lala's cheese, 27
Grusin, Dave, 185, 196
guacamole, Running-W-Bar, 94

H

ham, fresh, with 1,000 cloves of garlic,
    195

PHOTOGRAPHY CREDITS

Photographs copyright © 2006 by Tom Eckerle appear on the following pages: 1, 2, 15, 17, 19, 22, 24–25, 32, 37, 38, 41, 42, 48, 50, 51, 54–55, 56 (top and bottom), 61, 65, 69, 73, 78, 83, 88–89, 90, 92–93, 93 (right), 101, 104, 106, 113, 118–119, 124, 127, 129, 130, 137, 138, 140, 144–145, 147, 148, 151, 156–57, 159, 161, 162, 165, 169, 173, 178, 181, 186, 189, 190–191, 193, 194, 197, 199, 200, 205, 206, 211, 215

Photographs copyright © 2006 by Tom Murphy appear on the following pages: 5, 6, 8, 10–11, 12, 18, 21, 31, 34–35, 43, 44–45, 58, 60, 63, 66–67, 70, 76–77, 81, 84, 85, 86, 87, 96–97, 98–99, 102, 103, 110–111, 116, 117, 120–121, 132–133, 134, 143, 166–167, 170–171, 176–177, 182, 202–203

Photographs copyright © 2006 by Ken Regan/Camera 5 appear on pages 14 and 164

Photographs on pages 13, 16, 28, 29, 40, 126, 142, 183, 185, courtesy of the authors